A Teen Girl Answers Darwin

Why You Are God's Amazing Creation and Not an Accident of Evolution

Kelvin Chan

Raisealife Canada

Sometimes, it takes a child to tell it like it is and expose the lies people believe. Sometimes, an imaginative dream can lead us to reflect on bedrock truths we need to build our lives on. In *A Teen Girl Answers Darwin,* author Kelvin Chan encourages readers to embrace their God-given identity and purpose and to believe and speak the truth—no matter how uncomfortable that may be. *A Teen Girl Answers Darwin* is much more than an imaginative story. In the following sections, the reader is encouraged to check out the evidence for the truth claims in the story. Kelvin Chan has done his research! I heartily recommend this book to readers of all ages.

Pastor Rick Powell
Collingwood Baptist Church, Vancouver, BC
Canada

Preface

Welcome to *A Teen Girl Answers Darwin!* This book begins with a story about a teenage girl taken on a surreal journey. Along the way, she discovers inspiration for her upcoming valedictory speech. After this initial chapter, the book explains key elements of the story and answers crucial questions relating to how God created each of us.

The pages will present insights from scientists, engineers, and even presidents. They will tell you about Nobel Prizes awarded for breakthrough discoveries that shed light on our origins. Most importantly, you will learn how these discoveries support our creation by God rather than by evolution.

In many chapters, callout boxes will direct you to carefully selected online videos and articles. I encourage you to check out this supplementary material. Watching videos is an easy and enjoyable way to appreciate the creative genius of God. It will also deepen and cement your understanding.

I pray this book takes you on a journey and brings you home to where all Bible-believing Christians belong. Moreover, I pray this book gives you an unwavering conviction that we are God's amazing creation.

Thank you for allowing me to share it with you.

I dedicate this book to my paternal grandmother, Ching Lim, who made her way to Victoria, British Columbia, Canada in 1911. It is my thanks to her for teaching me the Bible when I was a child.

I also dedicate this book to the courageous professors and scientists who take the difficult path to teach the truth. Some of these individuals are noted within this book. I extend my appreciation to all for their commitment to sharing their knowledge.

Contents

A Teen Girl Answers Darwin

And it shall come to pass afterward, that I will pour out my Spirit on all flesh; your sons and your daughters shall prophesy, your old men shall dream dreams, and your young men shall see visions.

Joel 2:28

Introduction

The following story was inspired by a girl named
Chantal, who once stood out as the valedictorian of
her Grade 7 class. Years later, she became the worship
leader at her church, displaying the same dedication
she showed as a student. Chantal delivered her Grade
7 speech barefoot, a moment that lives on in my
memory.

Chapter 1

The Dream

It was the day of my Grade 7 graduation. A whirlwind of emotions engulfed me. Amidst the honor of being chosen class valedictorian, it was the final farewell to my beloved elementary school, Christina Johnson Elementary. With impending goodbyes, a deep sense of loneliness crept in. For some inexplicable reason, after tonight, all my classmates and friends of my past seven years will never see each other again.

But how could that be? The thought of never seeing my closest friends again made my eyes well up.

I was only 12 years old, torn between the excitement of graduation and the overwhelming desire to hold onto the only faces I had ever known. The impending farewell felt like an impossible task for someone so young. How could I put on a happy face when every cell of my body wanted to cry: "No! I don't want this to be goodbye!"

As I contemplated what to say, a somber mood enveloped me. The prospect of addressing not only my friends, but their parents and all the teachers weighed heavily on me. The enormity of the moment made it difficult for me to breathe. In a treacherous storm, I was at its center, surrounded by waters that threatened to swallow me.

In an instant, my world collapsed into darkness. I tumbled backward through a sea of white clouds. My eyes gently closed, and my muscles surrendered to weightlessness.

As I continued freefalling through the air, the crushing weight that had burdened me gradually dissipated. A gentle calm returned to my breathing. Opening my eyes, I found myself standing on my feet, wandering through a dense white fog. The damp air was thick, obscuring my vision to the point where only shapeless shadows and fleeting light passed me by.

From the heavy, curling mist, a rather large, portly man materialized. Like a large, inflated punching clown, he radiated an aura of friendliness without uttering many words. "Let's go for a drive," he suggested.

Without a hint of fear, I decided to trust him. Opening the back door of a sprawling white car, he said: "Come."

As I settled into the soft leather back seat, the man took the wheel, and we embarked on a silent journey. As we hit the highway, a surreal scene unfolded. Instead of cars, bizarre-looking animals raced alongside us. One creature caught my eye, a peculiar blend of a donkey and a horse. Its head, neck, and front legs resembled a donkey; while its rear end, back legs, and tail mirrored those of a horse—the mismatched anatomy made for awkward strides.

Other fantastical creatures paraded by. A white mountain goat's head, adorned with curved, black horns, and the front legs of a mountain goat were fused onto the body of a wooly sheep. It tried to leap gracefully like a goat, only to crumple to the ground upon landing.

Amidst this bewildering scene, I couldn't shake the question, *Where on earth am I?*

The car veered off the highway onto a weathered dirt road cocooned by towering trees. The dense forest engulfed us, casting a foreboding darkness broken only by the narrow strip of road ahead. For a moment, an unwelcome thought popped into my head. *No one knows where I am, and I am deep in the forest with a stranger.*

Just as the gloomy, shadowless surroundings seemed endless, the car emerged into a bright clearing. Getting out of the car, we stood high above a breathtaking lake surrounded by majestic mountains and a sea of green trees. To my astonishment, this was the lake where our class had experienced our most memorable field trip.

In a blink, I found myself transported back in time, reliving that sun-drenched day. My entire class was gathered at the lake, our joy echoing through the air. Some splashed in the water, others scaled rocks or reclined under the sun's warmth. As the sun's rays warmed our bodies, we gazed at the sky and clouds, enjoying the sight of white bunnies and other fluffy creatures overhead. Some of us etched our names onto the boulders. We wanted future visitors to know that we were there.

The scene unfolded like a vivid painting, and a realization dawned on me: what I was seeing was meant to inspire my upcoming speech. The happiness of that moment enveloped me, tempting me to linger and bask in its warmth. However, the man, ever so mysterious, declared it was time to move on.

Back in the car, we bounced our way through the dark forest again. Before long, we arrived at another clearing. Pulling up to a modest one-story cottage adorned with a simple front garden, my driver came to a stop. He opened the car door, gesturing for me to follow. "Come," he uttered quietly.

Approaching the unassuming front door, I saw there was no need to ring the doorbell. My driver effortlessly swung the door open, inviting me to step inside.

The interior was sparsely furnished—no extravagant tiles or plush rugs. Warm sunshine streamed through a window, casting a gentle glow on a young girl. She was playing on the wooden plank floor. Barely a year and a half old, she was all by herself yet displayed no trace of fear as I approached.

Spotting a doll nearby, I picked it up and presented it to her. With a radiant smile, she accepted the offering. We exchanged no words, yet a contented silence enveloped us as if everything that needed to be communicated was understood without speech. Once again, I felt an overwhelming desire to stay in the moment. However, my mystery man intervened, declaring it was time to move on.

As he swung the door open to let us exit, he echoed the familiar invitation: "Come."

Once again, we settled into the car, venturing through the mysterious depths of the dark forest. Time seemed to stretch endlessly as we journeyed. Resting my head on the soft comfort of the car seat, I surrendered to the gentle rocking motion and closed my eyes. The car became a cocoon, cradling me into a soothing, restful sleep.

I stirred as the car came to a halt. However, to my surprise, it wasn't just the driver and me in the white car. My dad's hands firmly gripped the steering wheel, my mom elegantly dressed beside him, and my little brother nestled at my side. The vehicle had brought us to a familiar place—the parking lot of Christina Johnson Elementary.

I observed the arrival of my friends and their families, their anticipation mirroring our own. As I stepped into the school's gym, the atmosphere buzzed with excitement. Instead of a mundane cavernous room, floodlights bathed the walls in vibrant purple, pink, and blue hues. Long, curled ribbons and delicate flower petals adorned the room, while stars glowed magically from the ceiling.

My classmates appeared remarkably grown up, the girls donning dresses and heels, their hair made up. The boys stood awkwardly in their crisp pants and white shirts. We couldn't help but steal glances at each other. Captivated by the transformation of our once-familiar gym into a dazzling celebration space, we could feel the air charged with a sense of excited anticipation.

Once we had all settled into our designated chairs, the school principal took the stage, extending her warmest welcome to all our families. She proudly acknowledged us, the Grade 7 graduates, as the most exceptional class in all her years as a school principal. With confidence, she expressed her belief that our journey would continue successfully in high school and beyond—in our future careers, both in our city and the world.

Following her, the president of the Parent-Teacher Association stepped forward, delivering a heartfelt speech. Her words dripped with gratitude as she thanked the dedicated teachers for their tireless efforts in teaching and caring for us as if we were their own children. By this time, many of us had become teary-eyed as well.

Then, a hush fell over the room as the principal announced the next speaker—the Grade 7 class valedictorian. The air tingled with anticipation, marking the moment we had all been waiting for.

A sudden surge pulsed through me, my heart beating faster. Muscles tensed as I rose from my seat. Adorned with a slight smile, I ascended the steps to the podium. The unfamiliar height of my new black high-heeled shoes pulsed discomfort through my feet.

Facing the gathered families, I decided to free my feet from the confines of my shoes. Instant relief washed over me. As my bare feet settled on the solid wooden floor, a newfound strength coursed through my body, dispelling any lingering traces of anxiety.

With a steady breath, I placed the sheet of paper containing my speech on the podium. My speech was going to be unlike any they had ever heard. Some teachers may even be angry. But it was a message I needed to deliver—because I would never see my classmates again.

As a warm spotlight bathed me in light, I began my speech.

Dear teachers, parents, family members, and my incredible fellow students! I am so honored to be here this evening to stand before you to represent the Grade 7 graduating class.

Many of us have known each other for half our lives. We have worked hard, played, and gone on field trips together. We celebrated birthdays and even fought together. And we are all so proud to be here tonight.

As this is our graduation, we will leave Christina Johnson Elementary and grow up to become adults. Like caterpillars that become butterflies, we will spread new wings. Our good times from elementary school will soon become distant, cherished memories as we go to different schools.

We will be leaving the one world that we know so well to enter a new, unfamiliar world. Each of us will forge our own path. So what do I say to all of you as we leave? What words can meaningfully send us on our way as we cross the divide into the rest of our lives?

My dear fellow students, the first thing I want to share with you is this: *You were created by God!*

As you grow up, you will repeatedly hear about Darwin and evolution. Scientists and the media will endlessly portray our lives as just a remarkable accident of nature. Billions of years ago, they say, lightning hit a warm pool of mud. Chemicals in the mud formed into a living cell. That single cell, like bacteria, over the years, became a worm. Over more years, it became a mouse, a monkey, and finally, a man and a woman. They will tell you that Charles Darwin discovered how we arose from the mud to become humans and that evolution created all the beautiful plants and animals on our planet.

But I would like to tell you more.

If we go back to the 1800s, when Charles Darwin lived, science was rudimentary. In those days, people thought fleas arose from dust if their homes were dirty. Baby fleas didn't need parents! So, it's not surprising that Darwin would propose that humans descended from tiny worms.

Darwin didn't really know much about humans at all. He didn't have the slightest idea about what was in the cells of our body. For Darwin, each cell was just a blob of jelly. I guess you could say he would think that we are all just billions of jelly blobs!

Fast forward to today, science has transformed our world and our understanding of the human body. In our science textbook, we read that each cell of our body contains DNA. It was only in 1953—when my grandpa was born—that two brilliant scientists, James Watson and Francis Crick, unraveled the mystery of DNA. It is a code that tells your body how to make itself, giving you the characteristics you have, from your height to the color of your eyes and hair.

But because we today are growing up in the age of computer technology, we understand even more. It is plain to us that computer code is the foundation of computer software. So it's only our generation that can fully appreciate the incredible scientific discovery that DNA is a sophisticated form of computer code!

Does that sound unbelievable? Well, if you talk to Bill Gates, the founder of Microsoft, he will tell you that DNA is far more advanced than any software ever created.

Yes. Have you heard that we will soon implant computer chips in people's brains? Well, there's already even more advanced programming in every cell of our bodies! And remember when we learned that computer code was all about 1s and 0s? Well, DNA encodes much more information as it uses four characters instead of just two.

Consider this for a moment. Software programmers write computer code. Like baby fleas, computer code doesn't come from dust in our homes. And in each of our cells, there are 3 billion characters of complex code. That makes us walking, breathing testaments of advanced biological programming!

Even more mind-blowing are the unbelievably tiny molecular machines in our cells. They read the DNA code to manufacture your body's tissues! Yes, you heard me right! Miniature living machines in your cells create your body! Our very existence is intricately encoded and manufactured at a microscopic level.

I'm going to repeat it. You were created by God! Only God could write the 3 billion characters of code that you had when you were just an egg inside your mother. Only God could engineer tiny nano-sized machines to read that code to build the handsome guys and beautiful girls you are today.

My dear fellow students. Remember the epic field trip to the lake where we had an absolute blast? A day that we will cherish forever when we look back on our Grade 7 year? We all wanted to leave our mark, whether it was carving our names on a tree stump or scratching them on a rock. We wanted to shout out: "Hey, we were here!"

Guess what? God wanted to leave a mark, too, but he didn't settle for a casual "I was here!" Nope. He went all out and wrote an entire book—the Bible! Incredible, right? That's the second thing I want to share. I know the principal and teachers might not be too thrilled about me saying this. But here's the scoop: back in the early years of Christina Johnson Elementary, the Bible was read aloud every morning.

Let's consider the Bible for a moment.

First off, God orchestrated its creation. He inspired a bunch of people to jot down the words, turning it into a collection of books. It's like God's way of shouting from the mountaintops, "Hey, I was totally here!"

But it's not just divine graffiti. It's the ultimate guidebook. It reveals the secrets of where we came from and offers a roadmap on how best to live our lives. It also clues us in on the incredible promises that God has in store for us. It's the ultimate life handbook from our Creator Himself!

Picture this: God, the ultimate artist, created you as a masterpiece. He made each of us a unique and awe-inspiring work of art. Imagine strolling through a museum in Florence, Italy, gazing up at Michelangelo's magnificent statue of David.

Well, here's the kicker: God sees you as an even more incredible masterpiece than that statue. He intricately wove three billion characters of code into every cell of your body. He gave you life. He made you a living masterpiece with unique abilities. And He wants you to create a wonderful life with it.

So, as we leave Christina Johnson and go out to discover life, there's a crucial guide waiting for us: the Bible. It's not just any book; It's a precious gift from God Himself. If you don't read it, it is like receiving a beautifully wrapped present and never bothering to unwrap it to discover what awaits you. It's your guide to crafting a life that is rich with purpose and meaning.

The Bible is also full of captivating stories. One of my favorites is a story about a woman named Ruth and her Jewish mother-in-law, Naomi. You know how people joke about tensions between women and their mothers-in-law? Well, in this story, Ruth and her mother-in-law are different.

In a foreign land, Ruth and Naomi suffer the harsh trials of life. They lose everything. Both of Naomi's sons die, leaving Ruth without a husband. But despite these difficulties, a remarkable, loving bond forms. In a touching declaration, Ruth tells Naomi, "Wherever you go, I will go, and where you lodge, I will lodge. Your people shall be my people, and your God my God."

After a long journey on foot to Naomi's hometown of Bethlehem, Naomi teaches Ruth how to meet a good man who will genuinely care for her. To cut a long story short, it concludes with a happy ending. And today, the words "ruth" and "ruthless" have their origins in this story. The word "ruth" embodies "love and caring," and "ruthless" is the absence of it. Read this heart-warming story for yourself before it gets made into a movie.

Another inspiring story is about a woman named Esther. In this story, a king chooses a stunningly beautiful virgin named Esther as his new queen. But because of anti-Semitism, Esther hides her Jewish heritage. Then, one day, an evil advisor to the king hatches a diabolical plan to wipe out all the Jews in the kingdom. As the king's queen, Esther is the only person who can prevent this catastrophe. How? By going to the king uninvited and revealing that she is also a Jew and pleading for the lives of her people.

But here's the catch. The king has a horrible rule. She can only visit him when he sends for her. If she approaches him without his invitation, her life could be on the line! Yes, it's a terrible rule, but that's how kings operated in those days. Esther, armed with unbelievable courage, sees the king without a formal invitation and saves her people.

Dear fellow students, as we step into the great adventure of life, let these two stories be our compass. Like Esther, in critical moments, embrace the kind of courage needed to do what is right. And like Ruth, no matter what trials we encounter, remember to bring care and compassion to the people around you.

Finally, a stupendous story. The Bible tells us about a series of incredible events in the life of a girl named Mary. Mary is single, but she's engaged to this guy, Joseph. And before they can tie the knot, Joseph discovers that Mary's pregnant.

But wait, it's not your typical reality show meltdown. Instead of creating a public scandal, Joseph surprises us. Brace yourself—he still loves Mary. Unbelievable, right? He decides to call off the engagement but to do it quietly, not wanting to hurt Mary's reputation. Now, that's a guy I would be honored to meet! By the way, Mary didn't cheat on Joseph. Her baby was a miracle of God!

Believe it or not, the story doesn't end there. Instead of breaking up, Mary and Joseph stay together, welcoming a baby into the world. The baby's name is Jesus. And because of this baby, we now say our year is 2026, which is 2,026 years since he was born. Even more importantly, because of Jesus, we now have hospitals! And we have universities! And even our favorite time of the year, Christmas! Like, can you imagine life without Christmas?

The story is so mind-blowing that you'll want to grab the Bible and uncover the rest of the twists and turns. Because I'm not going to tell you anymore, and the ending always surprises everyone. But hey, you're just graduating from Grade 7, and your adventure has only just begun.

Alright, as we bid a fond farewell to Christina Johnson Elementary and step into the whirlwind of growing up, I want to leave you with two crucial thoughts.

First, do you remember the story from your primary grades, "The Emperor's New Clothes?" A devious tailor spins a supposedly "invisible" suit for the emperor, convincing him he is decked out in fine clothes that he can't see. And then all the adults, terrified of getting into trouble, nod their approval and praise the non-existent outfit. It takes an innocent little kid, blissfully unaware of potential consequences, to blurt out the truth: "The emperor isn't wearing any clothes!"

This is the first story of political correctness. As you grow up, don't be a parrot for the sake of being politically correct. Speak the truth like that little kid, even if it means ruffling a few feathers.

Yes, it isn't politically correct to say that God created you. Some "adults" may even want you to swear to being a distant grandchild of a worm or a monkey before accepting you in their circle. But channel the innocence of the little child in the story of "The Emperor's New Clothes." Resist the urge to go along with the ridiculous. Have the courage to believe and speak the truth, even if it's not popular. Because sometimes, going against the grain is where real courage lies.

Follow the evidence wherever it leads. Read about the incredible world of DNA and why Bill Gates says DNA is like a computer program, though far more advanced than any software ever created. When one of the world's top computer industry experts says it's reasonable to believe in God, it's worth paying attention. Believe in the sensible, like Bill Gates, and stay clear of unreasonable ideas that say your distant great-great-great-grandparents were worms and monkeys.

And for the second crucial thought I have for you, unwrap the incredible gift God has bestowed upon you. You are his amazing masterpiece with unique talents and abilities. Read the instruction manual for your life. Discover why Abraham Lincoln said, "I believe the Bible is the best gift God has ever given to man."

Thanks for being such a fantastic audience. As we venture into the next chapter of our lives—high school and beyond—I genuinely hope we see each other again. Here's to the exciting journey ahead, filled with truth, love and caring, and the courage to embrace the incredible masterpiece God created—You.

See what kind of love the Father has given to us,
that we should be called children of God; and so we are.

1 John 3

The Dream Unraveled

While dreams are often interpreted, this dream raises many questions. The following answers, online resources, and references will help you unravel this dream.

✳

It is the glory of God to conceal things,
but the glory of kings is to search things out.

Proverbs 25:2

Introduction

The next chapters will explain key themes and elements that were touched upon in "The Dream." We will start with the "The Story of DNA's Discovery" which is fundamental to the idea that humans were created by God.

Chapter 2

The story of DNA's discovery

In 1869, a Swiss doctor named Friedrich Miescher graduated from medical school. Interested in research, he moved to Tubingen, Germany, to work for a research lab. While investigating a type of blood cell in pus scraped off hospital bandages, he isolated a unique substance from the cell's nucleus. He named it "nuclein." Little did he know, he had discovered DNA, though what it was remained a mystery.

Jump ahead almost 50 years later to 1918. The world's deadliest pandemic, the Spanish flu, circled the globe. It killed an estimated 21 million people. However, most victims did not die from the flu virus. They died from bacterial pneumonia that invaded their damaged respiratory tracts and lungs. (The recent Covid-19 pandemic was similar. Most people died when they contracted pneumonia after the covid virus did its damage.)

Affected by the devastating deaths, Dr. Frederick Griffith, a British bacteriologist, decided to develop a pneumonia vaccine. In his laboratory, he grew two strains of the pneumococcus bacteria in plates of agar. When Griffith examined them under a microscope, one strain had a rough surface while the other looked smooth. So he named them "R" and "S" for rough and smooth, respectively.

He found that the rough R-strain was mild and did not kill the mice, while the smooth S-strain was lethal. The smooth S-strain, however, was harmless when Griffith killed it with heat. Once it was dead, injecting particles of it into mice did not make them sick.

However, in 1928, he told the world about a surprising experiment. When he added dead S-strain particles to live R-strain bacteria and injected both into the mice, the mice got pneumonia and died! The dead S-strain bacteria particles would change the live, harmless R-strain bacteria into deadly bacteria like the lethal S-strain.

This mysterious result, known as the "Griffith's Experiment," intrigued scientists. An American medical scientist, Dr. Oswald Avery, took on the challenge to solve the mystery. He and his Rockefeller Institute for Medical Research team dedicated themselves to finding the "transforming agent." After years of painstaking research, Dr. Avery's team found the answer. The DNA from the dead particles of killer S bacteria would transfer to and merge with the live, milder R bacteria. This transfer caused the harmless R bacteria to become lethal. In 1944, they announced their unexpected scientific breakthrough: DNA was genetic information. It could move from one bacterial cell to another. He called this process "bacterial transformation."

By the late 1940s, scientists suspected DNA was the genetic material that passed down inherited traits. But if this was true, *how* did DNA do this? It was another baffling mystery. No one could see what was inside DNA. It was like knowing that your computer's flash drive stored data, but how it did so, no one knew.

In 1950, a British biophysicist at King's College in London, Dr. Maurice Wilkins, joined the race to work on DNA. He determined how to purify it to a high concentration. Then, Dr. Rosalind Franklin, an expert in a new technique called X-ray diffraction, came on board. Together, they would develop methods to study matter at the molecular level. By exposing the long DNA thread to an X-ray beam, images showed shadows of DNA's parts. These shadows formed symmetrical patterns!

In the spring of 1951, an American geneticist, Dr. James Watson, met Dr. Wilkins at a Naples conference on X-ray crystallography. Inspired to join the hunt using the new X-ray technique, Watson got a position at Cavendish Laboratories at England's University of Cambridge. While there, he met Francis Crick, a Ph.D. student in theoretical physics. They decided to tackle the mystery of DNA together by building potential models of DNA's molecular structure.

As Dr. Franklin refined her images, Watson and Crick could slowly refine their models. In early 1953, they solved the puzzle after seeing one of Dr. Franklin's X-ray images. Crick would tell everyone they had discovered the secret of life! They had determined DNA's now famous double helix shape and its chemical structure. Watson and Crick published their discovery in the April 1953 edition of *Nature*.

Experiments by other scientists later confirmed their discovery. DNA was the carrier of genetic information needed for life.

In 1962, the Nobel Prize committee awarded prizes for Physiology or Medicine. The recipients were Dr. James Watson, Dr. Francis Crick, and Dr. Maurice Wilkins. (Sadly, the prize committee could not nominate Dr. Rosalind Franklin as she died from cancer in 1958.) The Nobel Prize Summary declared that they had determined that the specific order of the DNA code was a blueprint for "how information was transferred in living material" (cited from "Speedread: Deciphering Life's Enigma Code" by Joachim Pietzsch).

This newfound understanding of DNA transformed biology. Biologists could no longer think that living things were composed only of matter and energy. There was a third entity responsible for life, and it was *information*.

All life on earth requires genetic information. Without this information, life would cease to exist.

> Read the story of Dr. Oswald Avery and his team's discovery in an article called "DNA: The Transforming Principle and the Birth of Modern Genetics." Enter the article title in a Google search to find it.
>
> You can read the Nobel Prize summary for discovering DNA's structure in an article titled "Speedread: Deciphering Life's Enigma Code." Enter the title in a Google search.

Chapter 3

What is so surprising about how DNA works?

B asically, DNA works by storing *information in a digital form*. Four types of chemical subunits of DNA, called nucleotide bases,[1] form chemical codes that function like computer code. Their function lies in their "specific order" or "sequence" that becomes information. Thus, animals and humans (and other organisms) are more than just chemicals and chemical processes. They have information or instructional code within their cells!

A crucial part of the DNA information in each cell contains a specific type of code called *protein-coding* DNA. This critical code tells the body's cells how to build thousands of unique proteins using molecules called amino acids.

---

1. A nucleotide is a molecule that is the basic building block of Deoxyribonucleic Acid (DNA) and Ribonucleic Acid (RNA). Chemically, it consists of three components: a nitrogen-containing base (adenine, guanine, thymine, and cytosine in DNA, and adenine, guanine, uracil, and cytosine in RNA), a phosphate group, and a sugar molecule.

Why is this protein-coding DNA so important? Because proteins play two crucial roles. First, proteins are the building blocks of cells: muscle, skin, bones, hair, and every body part, organ, or tissue. Second, proteins run the biochemical processes that keep us alive. Take insulin, for instance, a key protein hormone that regulates our blood sugar level. It helps move glucose (sugar) into our cells. This regulation ensures our body has energy. Another example is hemoglobin, the protein in our red blood cells. It carries oxygen from the lungs to the rest of the body.

To build each protein, hundreds of amino acid molecules must combine. They form a long chain that folds into a unique shape. The amino acid molecules must be placed in a specific sequence or order. The DNA's instructional code determines the order. After the amino acid molecules join together in the correct order, they fold into a unique shape. They then become a functioning protein.

The DNA's instructional code must be accurate. For example, DNA must encode 574 amino acid molecules in a precise order to build the hemoglobin protein that carries oxygen to the body. Just one specific, incorrect amino acid in this complex chain causes sickle cell anemia, a severe and life-threatening blood disease!

After realizing that DNA is a long strand of code, the scientific community took on the challenge of decoding all the DNA in a human cell. The hope was that this effort would transform our understanding of biology, human health, and disease. The Human Genome Project[2] was a multi-country effort. Given a $3 billion budget, it began in 1990. Ten years later, on June 26, 2000, the U.S. White House held an international ceremony. It announced the completion of a remarkable feat—the mapping of human DNA's

---

2. A genome is a complete set of genetic material, including all the genes and DNA in an organism.

three billion characters.[3] President Bill Clinton declared, "Today, we are learning the language in which God created life."

See how amino acids become proteins and how proteins perform amazingly varied functions. Watch this YouTube video by Dr. Nathan Ahlgren, a professor of biology. It is called "What is a protein? A biologist explains." Find this video on the channel "The Conversation."

You can read more about the Human Genome Project, described as "the most important biomedical research undertaking of the 20th Century." Enter "Human Genome Project Fact Sheet" in a Google search to find it.

---

3. When the Human Genome Project ended in 2003, only 92% of the DNA was sequenced. New technologies were needed to read longer stretches of DNA. It took until 2022 to determine the order of the remaining characters. To read more, go to the website genome.gov/t2t.

Chapter 4

Do computer experts agree that DNA is sophisticated code?

Yes. Bill Gates is the co-founder of the software giant Microsoft. In his book *Road Ahead*, he explains that he was in his 20s when he read James Watson's book, *Molecular Biology of the Gene*. In *Road Ahead*, Bill Gates writes, "The understanding of life is a great subject. Biological information is the most important information we can discover.... DNA is like a computer program but far, far more advanced than any software ever created" (Viking Penguin, 1995, p. 188).

There are many ways in which DNA is more advanced than software programs in computers. One way is that computers use a "binary code" in which each digit can be "0" or "1." In contrast, DNA uses a "quaternary code" based on four chemical building blocks: adenine, thymine, guanine, and cytosine. These are commonly abbreviated as A, T, G, and C. This quaternary code allows DNA to pack much more information into the same number of digits when building instructional code.

DNA is not literally "computer code" because there is no physical computer. However, it represents a sophisticated, complex "natural code." It encodes and organizes vast amounts of information needed for biological processes.

With this new understanding, scientists studying molecular biology and genetics are starting to view life differently. Dr. James Shapiro is a Professor of Microbiology in the Department of Biochemistry and Molecular Biology at the University of Chicago. Writing about the complexity of how cells process information, he states that the complexity found in cells is like computer technology:[1]

> Upsetting the oversimplified views of cellular organization and function held at mid-century, the molecular revolution has revealed an unanticipated realm of complexity and interaction more consistent with *computer technology* than with the mechanical viewpoint which dominated the field when the neo-Darwinian Modern Synthesis was formulated. (italics added)

Dr. Shapiro points to DNA repair mechanisms. He says that they are examples of how cells operate like computer technology. These mechanisms proofread and correct errors during DNA copying processes.

Students studying cell biology at university will learn about *mismatch repair enzymes*. (Enzymes are proteins that enable biochemical processes.) These mismatch repair enzymes double-check the DNA code and correct errors. One enzyme called *mismatch recognition protein* identifies the DNA error. Once found, another enzyme snips out the section that contains the wrong code. Another enzyme inserts the proper code and seals

---

1. The quotation is from his 1997 article "A third way" in *Boston Review* 22 (1), 32-33.

the gap with the correct sequence. Mismatch repair is critically important. Persons born with defective mismatch repair enzymes can suffer serious illness. As they accumulate errors in their DNA, they increase their risk of cancer.

The discovery of mismatch repair enzymes is so significant that Dr. Paul Modrich, the James B. Duke Professor of Biochemistry at Duke University, received a Nobel Prize. He was awarded the 2015 Nobel Prize in Chemistry.[2]

Dr. Shapiro also notes that cells have molecular computing networks. They process information about what is happening inside and outside the cell. The network then decides how to control the cell's growth and how it moves. It may also change one type of cell into another type to make it perform different tasks.

> Watch a highly recommended video to appreciate the sophistication of DNA's code. It features Dr. Georgia Purdom, who holds a Ph.D. in molecular genetics and is a former biology professor. Her presentation is called "Wonder of DNA." This video, re-titled "Evolutionists Hate When You Bring This Up," is on the YouTube "Answers in Genesis" channel.

---

2. Dr. Modrich shared the 2015 Nobel Prize with two other researchers who worked on different mechanisms of DNA repair: Dr. Tomas Lindahl of the University of Gothenburg and Dr. Aziz Sancar of the University of North Carolina School of Medicine. You can read the Nobel Prize summary "The Cell's Toolbox for DNA Repair." Find it on the Nobel Prize webpage: www.nobelprize.org/prizes/chemistry/2015/press-release.

Chapter 5

Are there really 3 billion characters of code in our cells?

Yes...

In 2022, scientists completed the sequencing of human DNA. Based on this sequence, human DNA comprises 3,054,815,472 *base pairs.*[1] (A base pair refers to the pairing of two complementary chemical building blocks from adenine, thymine, cytosine, and guanine. Adenine always pairs with thymine, and cytosine always pairs with guanine.) Each base pair acts like a single text character.

---

1. This is the number of base pairs from the chromosomal DNA in the cell's nucleus. There are also 16,569 base pairs of DNA in the cell's mitochondria, which produce energy for the cell. (From the March 31, 2022 article "The Complete Sequence of a Human Genome" in Science, Volume 376, Issue 6588.)

To grasp the enormous amount of code within each of our cells, consider the King James English translation of the Bible. It has 3,116,480 characters.[2] That means the DNA in each human body cell is equivalent to 980 King James Bibles! (3,054,815,472 base pairs divided by the Bible's 3,116,480 characters = 980). Imagine the contents from a stack of 980 Bibles to comprehend the sheer volume of DNA's code!

The task would be monumental if you had to type all the characters of the human DNA. Assuming a typing rate of 60 words per minute, working 7 hours daily, five days a week, 52 weeks a year, it would take you *93 years*!

The National Human Genome Research Institute illustrates the amount of code in another way. They calculate that if you print the 3 billion letters of the human genome in size 12 font, it will stretch from Houston to Boston! That distance is about 1,600 miles!

No...

The human DNA is often said to be 3 billion characters long because the Human Genome Project aimed to map one complete DNA sequence. However, each person has a pair of chromosomes, threadlike structures of wound-up DNA—one from mom and the other from dad. Therefore, the number of DNA characters in humans totals 6 billion.

So now imagine that it would take you 186 years to type out the characters in the DNA of a single person!

However, there is a place in humans where there are only 3 billion characters, and that is in the mother's egg cells and the

---

2. The blog article titled "How many words in the Bible" can be found at wordcounter.net.

father's sperm cells. Once the sperm fertilizes the egg, the egg has two sets of chromosomes totaling 6 billion characters.

Sequencing the human DNA was a monumental task. It took 32 years. The project began in 1990 as the Human Genome Project, which ended in 2003. However, only 92% of the DNA was sequenced when the project ended. It was too difficult to continue. With the benefit of technological advances, scientists formed a new organization in 2019 to complete the work. It was called the Telomere-to-Telomere (T2T) Consortium. In 2022, the scientists announced they had completed the last 8%.

With the complete sequencing of the human DNA, we now know that all humans are 99.9% identical in their genetic makeup. The other 0.1% are variations that determine how we are unique. Our unique genetics determines our physical appearance, behavior, and susceptibility to certain diseases.

To read more details about DNA and genes, check out the Australian Academy of Science's webpage "All about DNA." Enter "Australian Academy of Science All about DNA" in a Google search to find it.

To read more on why it was such a difficult challenge to finish sequencing the complete human genome, go to genome.gov/about-genomics/telomere-to-telomere. Then scroll to "Infographic: Completing the human genome sequence."

Chapter 6

What are the implications of DNA being instructional code?

Code Requires an Author

Dr. Stephen Meyer explains the first implication. He says that everywhere in the world where there is information or instructional code, there is a mind or an intelligent source behind it. When people see letters forming words, a sentence, or a line of computer code, they immediately recognize that someone's mind created it. Therefore, Dr. Meyer concludes that DNA's code is evidence of an intelligent designer.

In 2009, he wrote *Signature in the Cell: DNA and the Evidence for Intelligent Design* (HarperCollins). This book describes the discovery of the digital code in DNA and the ramifications on the origin of life.

Evolutionary biologists argue that Dr. Meyer's conclusion is "unscientific." However, you can frame the counterargument to this perspective as follows. If you found an unsigned poem in your home, written in your father's poetry style, you could recognize his distinctive style. You would conclude that your father wrote it. And your father could confirm that it is his writing. Your reasoning does not rely on the principles of chemistry, biology, or physics. But your conclusion is correct. In the same way, Dr. Meyer's conclusion of an intelligent designer can also be correct. Science, based on physical processes, is not the arbitrator of truth in all situations.

The problem with evolutionary biologists is that they limit themselves. They will only explain things based on physical processes that science can observe. They will not consider the idea of a non-physical, intelligent designer who created genetic information. It simply falls outside the bounds of chemistry, biology, and physics.

While biologists will focus on the physical aspects of the "brain," we know that we also have a "mind" and we have emotions. We appreciate art, great music, and the beauty of nature. When evolutionary biologists dismiss specific ideas as "unscientific," they implicitly acknowledge that science cannot explain everything.

Considering that an intelligent source created DNA's complex code, we might ask, "Who made this extraordinary code?" Evolutionary biologists can never answer this question. Why? Because they are dedicated to explaining things through evolution. They will not consider other possibilities.

Code Does Not Evolve

The second implication deals with how DNA affects Darwin's theory of evolution. Darwin's theory of evolution says that random "variation" over time will generate new forms of life or new types of animals. And "natural selection" or "survival of the fittest" will determine which ones survive. However, with the discovery of the instructional code in DNA, Darwin's variation is not enough. We now know that something else is needed. If animals are to "evolve" new body parts and organs, there must be complex changes in DNA's genetic information.

When faced with the complexity of DNA's code, what do modern evolutionary biologists say? They say that DNA also evolved by natural selection! However, in today's computer age, many people understand programming. We know that errors in code (mutations) can never generate the additional complex code needed to build new functions. So common sense, based on our understanding of computer programming, tells us that DNA cannot simply evolve. We know that mutations will not create new types of functional organs (e.g., the human eye or an elephant's trunk) that have never existed before.

Mutations can, however, cause small changes that help an animal adapt to its environment. For instance, scientists think that the white polar bear might have descended from a brown bear that moved to the north. A simple mutation that made its fur white could help it survive. With a white coat, it can blend in with its ice-covered surroundings. However, mutations do not create entirely new organs or animals with completely different body shapes.

Evolutionary biologists, who ask you to believe that DNA's code just evolved, are asking you to suspend your judgment and trust them. Their claim is merely a speculative attempt to explain away persuasive evidence of creation by a higher intelligence.

Like the child in the story "The Emperor's New Clothes," you do not need to accept, uncritically, the claims of evolutionary biologists. You do not have to accept their assertion that complex code can magically write itself. Instead, trust your judgment about what you know about the world. Information is a sign of an intelligent mind.

Chapter 7

Do molecular machines in our cells really create our body?

Yes. We have incredibly tiny machines in our cells. When we think of machines, we might think of machines in factories that make parts for cameras or kitchen appliances. Typically, these machines are made of metal and need an energy source, such as electricity, to make them work.

In our cells, however, the machines are intricate biological molecules. They are typically made of *protein complexes*. Protein complexes are two or more protein molecules that work together to perform a specific task. Like the machines in factories, the machines in our cells consume energy.

The tiny machines in our cells can do an astounding variety of functions. They can cut material, select the required parts, bond components together, and break down damaged parts for recycling. They can pump liquids and be valves to control fluids. They move. They can even build new machines.

Most importantly, molecular machines read, copy, and process DNA's instructional code to create your body!

To create a new human being, a man's sperm cell fertilizes a woman's egg cell. This fertilized egg cell contains the complete set of genetic material, or DNA, from both the father and the mother. Two things must happen for this fertilized egg to grow into a baby. First, the single cell must constantly grow by rapidly dividing itself millions of times until it forms an embryo. Over about eight weeks, all the major organs and body systems develop, although not fully formed. Between eight weeks and the baby's birth, the fetus continues to grow and mature until it is a fully formed baby.

From the initial fertilization of the egg to the development of a fully formed baby, molecular machines in the cells perform two vital tasks. To split a cell into two identical "daughter cells," DNA must duplicate itself. Then each daughter cell will have a complete copy of the original genetic information. Molecular machines perform this copying, which is called "DNA replication."

During cell division, cells must also create proteins because they are the building blocks of new cells and tissues. Molecular machines select different amino acids and join them together in a precise order. This process is called "protein synthesis."

Cell Division

When a DNA strand needs to copy itself so a cell can split into two, each with its DNA, many molecular machines do the work. But two are notable. The first, called *DNA Helicase*, is a molecular motor. It unwinds the double-stranded DNA molecule into two single strands. The second is the molecular machine called *DNA Polymerase*. It adds the new chemical building blocks (A, T, G, and C) to each newly separated strand, resulting in two double-stranded DNA molecules.

This process reveals that our body's cells not only have sophisticated instructional code, but they also have sophisticated, machine-based information processing!

A medical research institute called WEHI (The Walter and Eliza Hall Institute of Medical Research) creates computer animations for the human body. Their 3D computer-generated animations show how these incredible molecular machines work.

Watch their video "DNA Replication 2010" to see how DNA Helicase unwinds the double-stranded DNA molecule into single strands. Find it on the YouTube "WEHImovies" channel by searching for "DNA Replication 2010."

Watch their video "DNA Polymerase 2010" to see how DNA Polymerase adds new chemical building blocks (A, T, G, and C) to the unwound single strands. Find it on the "WEHImovies" channel by searching for "DNA Polymerase 2010."

Protein Synthesis and Two Nobel Prize-Winning Discoveries

We all know that we eat food to supply our bodies with energy and to grow. Surprisingly, it has only been in the last 25 years that scientists have discovered the role of DNA and our cells' molecular machines. Our DNA and cells' molecular machines take the digested food we eat to create the proteins needed to build our body's tissues.

When we eat proteins from our food, the body's digestive system breaks the protein down into chemicals called amino acids. These amino acids pass through the intestinal walls into the bloodstream. The blood can then carry them to the body's cells. There are 20 different amino acids used to form new proteins. Our body can synthesize 11 of them (called *non-essential amino acids* because our body makes them). The remaining nine come from the food we eat (called *essential amino acids* because we need to eat to get them). The mystery is this: How do our cells reconstitute the amino acids into the thousands of unique proteins used in the body?

Scientists know that a vital portion of DNA, known as protein-coding DNA, contains the blueprints for arranging amino acids. But the first question is: How does the DNA code even get read?

It was not until 2001, after three decades of research, that Dr. Roger Kornberg made this critical scientific discovery. He showed how *RNA polymerase II*, a molecular machine, extracts genetic code from DNA. In a process called *transcription*, this machine transcribes the code. It reads the DNA and rewrites it as a template for further processing.

What happens is this. First, the RNA polymerase II binds to the DNA, where the protein-coding information is located. It separates the two DNA strands. Then, it moves along the strand, extracting and recording all the information from the DNA. This creates a molecule called mRNA. This mRNA is a template of the DNA. The mRNA then exits the cell nucleus and finds its way to the home of large molecular machines called *ribosomes* in the cell's watery interior. In computer technology terms, the mRNA is like a flash or thumb drive that transfers data to another location.

Dr. Kornberg won the 2006 Nobel Prize in Chemistry for his discovery of how DNA is read.

From the 1970s to the early 2000s, Dr. Venkatraman Ramakrishnan, Dr. Thomas A. Steitz, and Dr. Ada E. Yonath researched ribosomes. Ribosomes are the molecular machine factories that make proteins. The three scientists discovered how ribosomes use the mRNA to assemble amino acids to become proteins.

What do ribosomes do? Ribosomes read the mRNA template and make whatever was originally encoded by the DNA. They move along the mRNA template and, acting like miniature knitting machines, select amino acids one by one and bond them together. This process forms *polypeptide chains* (the term for amino acids joined by peptide bonds). These chains then fold themselves into proteins that have specific functions in the body.

Translation is the term for using the mRNA template to arrange amino acids to form proteins. That is because it "translates" genetic information into physical components of life—proteins! The body then uses the newly created proteins to build its tissues or perform the biochemical processes of life.

Dr. Ramakrishnan, Dr. Steitz, and Dr. Yonath won the 2009 Nobel Prize in Chemistry for their work on the ribosome and its role in making proteins. This 2009 Nobel prize, Dr. Roger Kornberg's 2006 prize for discovering the transcription process, and Drs. Watson, Crick, and Wilkins' 1962 prize for their discovery of the structure of DNA are three pivotal awards.

These three Nobel Prize-winning discoveries are momentous. Combined, they explain how DNA's sophisticated code and molecular machines create living things. They profoundly affect our understanding of genetics and the nature of our world.

Many people have now heard of mRNA due to receiving an mRNA vaccine for the Covid virus. In an mRNA Covid vaccination, a person's arm gets an injection of mRNA particles. The mRNA enters the cells and travels to ribosomes, which use the mRNA information to create Covid proteins. The person's immune system then reacts to the internally created Covid proteins. In mounting a defense against these Covid proteins, the body builds immunity to infection from the Covid virus.

Watch how ribosomes create proteins in the WEHI animation called "Ribosome." Find it on the YouTube "WEHImovies" channel by searching for "Ribosome."

Read about the two Nobel Prize awards. The award summary for Dr. Roger Kornberg's 2006 Nobel Prize in Chemistry is titled "The DNA Reader in Our Cells." Find it at www.nobelprize.org by searching for "The DNA-Reader in Our Cells."

You can read more about Dr. Venkatraman Ramakrishnan, Dr. Thomas A. Steitz, and Dr. Ada E. Yonath's Nobel Prize contributions in this article called "The Key to Life at the Atomic Level." Find this article by entering the article name into a Google search.

Chapter 8

Why evolutionary biologists dislike molecular machines

Evolutionary biologists are not keen to talk about molecular machines. Why?

First, the presence of molecular machines is a severe problem for Darwin's theory. To explain why, Darwin's theory of evolution says that advanced life forms, such as cats and monkeys, evolved from simpler life forms, such as ancient worm-like creatures. The theory says that complex organs and structures, like the eyes in cats, developed slowly over millions of years. It supposedly happened through "numerous, successive, slight modifications" from simpler structures found in earlier life forms.

However, molecular machines are complex structures that cannot gradually form over time. For example, *DNA Polymerase* is the molecular machine that adds the chemical building blocks (A, T, G, and C) to the unwound single DNA strand to create a new strand. Building it requires arranging 775 amino acid molecules in a specific order. A machine made of 775 parts is complex!

Think of a mechanical wristwatch or a simple spring-loaded mouse trap. These devices would not work if even a single part were missing or deformed. Similarly, complex molecular machines are *irreducibly complex*. Dr. Michael Behe, a professor of biochemistry, coined this term in his book *Darwin's Black Box: The Biochemical Challenge to Evolution* (Free Press, 1996).

Dr. Behe explains that if something is irreducibly complex, it cannot have evolved through successive, slight modifications. All the parts must come together at the same time. If a machine existed in a less complex form, it would not work. Think of a clock missing just one gear. It would be incapable of telling time.

As molecular machines are irreducibly complex, they could not have evolved from simpler forms. Therefore, the existence of molecular machines is scientific evidence that Darwin's theory is wrong. Darwin says, "If it could be demonstrated that any complex organ existed, which could not possibly have been formed by numerous successive, slight modifications, *my theory would absolutely break down.*" (italics added, *On the Origin of Species*.[1] 1st ed., 1859 reprint, Bantam, 1999, p. 158). Molecular machines are the evidence that breaks his theory!

Second, what defines something as a machine? A "machine" is a complex device *designed* to perform a specific task. Because a machine is complicated, no one would expect it to create itself by chance. So, just as we can infer that DNA's instructional code must come from an intelligent source or a mind, we can also reasonably assume that molecular machines must be designed or engineered by an intelligent source or mind.

In our modern age, we now marvel at the technology of 3D printers. They can make physical products by extruding layers of plastic resin. The 3D printer is the marriage between a computer's

---

1. The full title of Darwin's book is *On the Origin of Species by Means of Natural Selection, or the Preservation of Favoured Races for the Struggle of Life.* For brevity, this will be shortened to *On the Origin of Species* or *Origin of Species* throughout this book.

instructional code and a machine that extrudes plastic. But way back in time, someone had an even more ingenious idea. Someone married instructional code with machines to build something better—the parts of our bodies!

Listen to Dr. Jonathan McLatchie's podcast "Jonathan McLatchie on Classic Examples of Irreducibly Complex Systems." Dr. McLatchie holds a Ph.D. in evolutionary biology. In this podcast, he explains how DNA replication requires multiple molecular machines, and together, they comprise an irreducibly complex system. He describes the function of each molecular machine and how, if any single machine is missing, cells will not divide or replicate. Find this podcast on the YouTube channel "Discovery Science."

To quote Dr. McLatchie, "Darwin got it wrong....We now understand the information basis of life; we understand that molecular machines run the show in biology."

Chapter 9

Isn't there a lot of fossil and anatomical evidence for evolution?

Evolutionary scientists point to fossil and anatomical evidence to support Darwin's theory of evolution. But their arguments are based on a mistaken assumption. They assume that similar structures found in different species are evidence of evolution.

An example is the best-selling book *Your Inner Fish: A Journey Into the 3.5-Billion-Year History of the Human Body* (Vintage, 2009). This book is written by Dr. Neil Shubin, a paleontologist and professor of anatomy. Dr. Shubin describes fossils and DNA, and how our hands resemble a type of fossilized fish fin. He uses this resemblance as evidence that humans evolved from fish. (There are several YouTube videos in which Neil Shubin explains his work.)

Scientists call similar anatomical structures between different species *homologies*. A whale fin with five digits is said to be homologous to a man's hand, which also has five digits. Evolutionary biologists see this as evidence that one species came from another. They conclude that we share a common ancestor. But, such homologies may be a sign of something entirely different.

For a moment, let us imagine a future Earth where humans have disappeared and aliens land on the planet. They see no people. But among the deserted cities, the aliens see bicycles, motorcycles, cars, and buses. Comparing the structure of these objects, they see that all have wheels, frames, and seats. The aliens conclude that bicycles must have evolved into motorcycles. Motorcycles then evolved to become cars and buses. However, this conclusion is incorrect. It misses a crucial factor in the explanation. Humans designed each of these vehicles. Humans used similar parts and principles from the earlier inventions of bicycles.

The observations that organisms have similar structures are correct. However, the conclusion that homologous anatomical features are proof of evolution is incorrect. We should listen to Dr. Stuart Burgess, Professor of Engineering Design at the University of Bristol, to understand why.

Dr. Burgess has spent 30 years teaching mechanical design. His expertise was recognized in 2019 when he was awarded the prestigious James Clayton Prize. This prize is awarded for outstanding contributions to mechanical engineering and related science, technology, and invention. His career included designing the 14-meter-long solar array of ENVISAT, the world's largest earth observation satellite. He also published over 200 scientific papers on the science of design. He is also passionate about *bio-inspired design*. Bio-inspired design involves creating innovative designs by studying plants and animals.

In a podcast titled "The Pentadactyl Whale Flipper: An Engineering Masterstroke," Dr. Burgess presents a compelling argument. He points out that the homology of the whale flipper and the human hand, often cited as evidence of evolution, is a weak, superficial argument. He argues that evolutionary biologists only point to visual similarities. They do not analyze the design of the whale flipper's bones. They do not ask why the flipper needs five bones. Perhaps a five-bone flipper is the best possible engineering design.

Dr. Burgess explains the function of the flipper. He explains that the flipper is a whale's control surface to maneuver its body while swimming in the ocean. It must change the flipper shape quickly to make sharp turns to pursue prey. While the flipper's five-bone structure is visually like a human hand, it is optimal for its purpose. This optimality would be consistent with the idea that the whale flipper resulted from engineering design.

Dr. Burgess argues that if evolutionary biologists believe the whale flipper bone structure is a leftover component adapted from a land animal, they should provide proof. They should show that there is a better engineering solution. That is, there is a potential flipper design that is better than one supposedly adapted from another animal.

He says that evolutionary biologists need to consider engineering design principles. Only then can they judge if something is designed or adapted from another species.

Dr. Burgess says that when evolutionary biologists point to similar structures in different species, they are actually showing evidence of purposeful design. He states, "In engineering, it is well-known that common designer gives common design." So, homologies signify that different animal species have the same designer.

> Listen to Dr. Burgess's podcast "The Pentadactyl Whale Flipper: An Engineering Masterstroke." You can find it online at the website address: https://idthefuture.com/1773/.

Chapter 10

Isn't survival of the fittest obvious?

Charles Darwin initially explained that evolution occurred through a process called "natural selection." Later, he changed the term from "natural selection" to "survival of the fittest."

The term "survival of the fittest" emphasizes that animals adapt to the environment in their struggle to survive. Those more successful at getting food, fighting off predators, and mating will survive and produce more offspring. Those that are less successful are less likely to survive and reproduce.

We can illustrate the concept of survival of the fittest in the following hypothetical example of a wooly sheep. Suppose, in a colder climate, sheep with thicker wool coats could endure the cold and continue to reproduce. Sheep with thinner coats would die from the cold. Over time, sheep would evolve to have thicker coats. This part of Darwin's theory makes sense, and people can rightly say it is obvious.

However, in this example, the sheep remain sheep but have thicker coats. The sheep do not become a different species. The problem with the theory of evolution is that Darwin proposed that one kind of animal could become another animal or species if enough time passes. He believed simple organisms could become complex organisms with new anatomical features. Given enough time, in the order of millions of years, a bacterial cell would become a more sophisticated multicellular organism. It would later evolve to become a mouse, and on and on.

Darwin believed that the minor changes within existing species, which is obvious, given enough time, can lead to new organs and body plans, which is not at all obvious. Yet many intelligent scientists and even our friends believe in Darwin's theory. They believe that ancient bacteria became human beings.

But Darwin's argument is flawed. Let us again imagine that aliens come to Earth after humans have gone. One alien finds a recipe for banana-chocolate chip muffins and a metal box called an oven. Following the recipe, he mixes bananas, chocolate chips, flour, sugar, and eggs. He puts the mixture into the oven for 5 minutes, and nothing much happens. He increases the time to 10 minutes, and the mixture starts changing. After 20 minutes, the raw ingredients transform into a perfect banana-chocolate chip muffin. Oh, how delicious! It tastes so good that he says, "Let's keep it in the oven for an entire month and see what we will get."

Does it become a banana cream pie? A chocolate cheesecake? Or does it become a dry, tasteless, hard lump?

This simple analogy illustrates three points. The first is that one cannot assume a change in a short time period will translate into a greater or better changes over a longer time period. (Doing so invites what scientists call an extrapolation error.)

Second, a banana-chocolate chip muffin cannot become a banana cream pie. A banana cream pie needs additional ingredients. Similarly, higher-level animals need different chemical components, organs, and physiological processes than simpler organisms.

The crucial third point is that what comes out of the oven is determined by the recipe, a specific type of information. In the same way, the instructional code in DNA is our recipe. The recipe that is the code in DNA determines what kind of animal or human being is created.

So, "survival of the fittest" in a limited way makes sense. It explains why some subgroups within a species develop slight differences from others within the same species, like the example of sheep with thicker coats. Such small changes are called "microevolution." Survival of the fittest also explains why some animals, or species, die out. They can no longer survive environmental changes and become extinct. However, "survival of the fittest" creating new kinds of animals with entirely new organs over millions of years—often called "macroevolution"—is implausible.

Charles Darwin was a dedicated scientist. If Darwin had known that a "recipe" was written in DNA for each species, he might have come to different conclusions. Perhaps he would not have proposed that ancient, simple organisms evolved into human beings.

When people state that "survival of the fittest" is obvious, they overlook a critical part of Darwin's theory. Before "survival of the fittest" can occur, a process must generate new life forms *with new anatomical features*, even if those changes are minor. In the hypothetical example of sheep's wool thickness, the sheep population must already have some with regular coats while others have thicker coats. There must already exist what Darwin calls "variation."

At a fundamental level, variation makes sense. We see that within our own families. Each of us differs from our brothers and sisters. Today, most people understand genetics. Chromosomes and genes from our parents mix to create different combinations of features. We inherit some characteristics from our mother's genes and others from our father's.

However, we are still all human beings. This regular mixing of chromosomes never makes us into another species. How do we get from normal variation within family members to variation that generates new life forms with new anatomical features? How did the regular mixing of chromosomes create an elephant's trunk? How did a giraffe get its long neck?

Darwin acknowledged that he did not know why or how variation occurs when he wrote his book *Origin of Species*. He wrote his book a century before people understood genetics and DNA. Can evolutionary scientists, who now know about DNA's sophisticated code, justify Darwinian evolution? Can they explain how variations produce new species with new anatomical features, such as an elephant's trunk or a giraffe's long neck?

Modern evolutionary biologists believe genetic mutations cause more significant variations. Over millions of years, survival of the fittest will lead to remarkable changes. There will be new types of organs, bodies, and animal species. The problem for evolutionary biologists is that this is not plausible based on what we know about genetic mutations.

While minor genetic mutations can be harmless to the organism, many genetic mutations in animals lead to disease and death. Consider how computer code works. Modern cell phones are essentially computers that transmit data and do other tasks. Their microprocessor chips contain instructional code that determines their functions.

What happens if you have an early cell phone with a simple camera that can only take photographs, and you randomly change characters in its computer code? Either the camera will stop working, or its pictures will start looking strange (or possibly better if the colors are more intense). However, it is crucial to note that random changes in the cell phone's computer code will never turn the simple camera into a video camera that will record sound and moving images. A programmer must write new instructional code to create these new functions.

Instead of a cell phone camera, what happens in the human eye when mutations arise? Eye doctors today know that DNA mutations cause over 350 eye diseases, many of which lead to blindness. No mutations give people the extreme eyesight that eagles have, which can spot a small animal on the ground while soaring high in the sky.

Mutations are copying errors in genetic information. They are more often harmful rather than beneficial. Indeed, even having the trait of blue eyes can be considered a harmful mutation for humans. In his book, *Darwin Devolves* (HarperOne, 2019), Dr. Michael Behe explains that people with blue eyes have a slight change in a gene called *OCA2*. This change results in losing the ability to produce the molecular pigment melanin in their eyes. Without this pigment, blue-eyed people are sensitive to bright lights.

Dr. Behe explains that DNA research has shown that mutations do not add genetic information to create new life forms. Instead, mutations degrade or damage existing genetic information. So, what happens when we breed dogs? Dr. Behe explains that, at the molecular level, the wide variety of dogs comes from degradative mutations. These mutations cause certain dog breeds to be more muscular, have long or curly fur, or even have friendly temperaments. In each case, the traits are attributed to breaking or degrading the normal genetic information rather than adding new genetic information.

He states, "Evolution can help make something look and act *different*, at least on the surface, but it doesn't have the ability to build or create anything at the genetic level." (italics added)

So, what Dr. Behe is saying is that mutations will change the characteristics of dogs. But they will always be dogs.

Chapter 11

What does the dream's image of a donkey-horse reveal?

In the dream, the class valedictorian takes a mysterious journey. In the car traveling on the highway, she sees bizarre-looking animals. One creature is a blend of a donkey and a horse. Its head, neck, and front legs resemble a donkey's; while its rear end, back legs, and tail mirror a horse's. So what is so special about a donkey and a horse blended together?

When you breed a female horse with a male donkey, you get an animal called a mule, which is highly valued as a work animal. Mules outperform horses in several ways. They can carry heavier loads, work for extended periods, and navigate rougher terrain. They have a longer lifespan and eat less food! Mules are also more intelligent than horses, although they can be stubborn. Mules have traits that would make them superior to horses, so it would be great if they could reproduce.

However, although we can create a mule by breeding a horse with a donkey, mules are sterile. Male and female mules cannot produce baby mules. In his book *Origin of Species*, Darwin discusses the interbreeding of two species, resulting in offspring that cannot reproduce. He states it is one of his theory's "gravest difficulties."

If mules were capable of reproduction, Darwin could have presented compelling evidence for the evolution of a new species from existing ones, specifically the horse and donkey. However, the infertility of mules is a severe problem for his theory. Why? Because evolution only occurs when animals reproduce. By reproducing, they show the emergence of a new species. There is no evolution without baby mules that grow up to mate and create a population of mules.

So, while Darwin *believes* that simple breeding of animals and the survival of the fittest can lead to new species, he cannot *show* this happening. A potential way—interbreeding—in which a new species with a new body form might emerge does not work.

Because interbreeding cannot produce new species, when evolutionary biologists are asked to give real-life examples of evolution, they point to breeding "within a species." They will say that, over time, selective dog breeding produces significantly different breeds, like huge Great Danes or tiny Chihuahuas. But the problem is that Great Danes and Chihuahuas are still dogs. They cannot breed dogs that grow horns on their heads or hooves on their feet like goats. They cannot produce a different type of animal.

According to the Bible, one should not breed one animal with a different kind of animal. As Leviticus 19:19 states, "You shall keep my statutes. You shall not let your cattle breed with a different kind." God believes that the created order is perfect and not to be tinkered with.

Mules cannot have babies for several genetic reasons. Watch this video called "Why Can't Mules Have Babies?" Find it on the YouTube "MinuteEarth" channel by searching for "Why Can't Mules Have Babies?"

Chapter 12

What do the dream's white bunnies in the sky signify?

In the dream, students enjoy a field trip to a lake on a beautiful sunny day. Many lie on their backs gazing at the clouds, seeing white bunnies and other fluffy creatures overhead. What does seeing white bunnies and fluffy creatures reveal about evolution? Seeing white bunnies is the reason people are predisposed to believe in evolution. Let me explain.

Our brains try to create meaningful patterns when we look at random shapes in clouds. Indeed, we enjoy finding animal shapes. This psychological phenomenon is called apophenia. Dr. Klaus Conrad, a professor of psychiatry and neurology, coined the term in 1958. He discovered it as he studied the "unmotivated seeing of connections" in his patients.

People enjoy "connecting the dots" to see meaningful patterns in everything. This human tendency can take several forms. One form is seeing patterns in "visual" phenomena or inanimate objects. For example, seeing bunnies when looking at clouds or seeing "a man in the moon."

Another form is perceiving meaningful connections in "events" or unrelated data. The most common examples are conspiracy theories. For instance, some individuals believe that the pharmaceutical industry created the Covid virus. They believe drug makers did it to earn money by selling vaccines.

Apophenia can also influence scientific research when scientists perceive patterns or relationships that do not exist. This cognitive bias then produces false conclusions or theories.

Paleontologists who see structural similarities in different species (e.g., a fossil fish fin and a human hand) are affected by apophenia. Looking at the pattern, they believe that fish evolved to become humans or had an earlier common ancestor. But this conclusion is wrong. They succumbed to the natural human tendency to perceive a meaningful pattern and drew an incorrect conclusion.

> To learn more about apophenia, read "Apophenia Explained: How to Avoid Apophenia Bias." You can find it by entering the title in a Google search.

A specific kind of apophenia is called *confirmation bias*. It is a big part of why people keep believing in evolution. Confirmation bias is the tendency to think something is true even when evidence is against it. It explains why evolutionary biologists continue supporting evolution. They continue even when discoveries such as molecular machines undermine Darwin's theory.

Confirmation bias is the reason why someone favors information supporting their beliefs. They also ignore or explain away information that goes against their beliefs. For instance, after people buy a new car, they will pay extra attention to ads and articles that confirm they made the right choice. You may even recognize yourself doing this. This tendency is normal human behavior.

As an example of confirmation bias affecting belief in evolution, we can look at scientists who conduct DNA research. Evolutionary biologists believe random mutations lead to evolution. So, they expect to find lots of random mutations or "junk" in DNA. They expect to see this randomness in the DNA that does not code for proteins. (Early scientists called this "junk DNA.") But, when new research shows that this DNA is not random junk, evolutionary biologists resist accepting the results. They resist because it goes against their evolutionary beliefs.

Another example of confirmation bias is scientists insisting that DNA must have evolved. During the Human Genome Project, researchers mapped 19,778 genes that code for proteins. This number comes from the Human Proteome Organization.[1]

Imagine making a single protein. You need a blueprint that tells you the exact order of hundreds of amino acids to make it. Without getting into mathematics, obtaining the correct order for one protein by chance alone would be incredibly improbable. Now, consider that there are almost 20,000 protein blueprints. It does not make sense to believe they all evolved by chance. It would be wishful thinking by those who want evolution to be true.

Confirmation bias affects evolutionary theorists. They choose to ignore the mathematical improbabilities that go against what they believe.

---

1. The Human Proteome Organization website, which cites the number of protein-coding genes, can be found at https://hupo.org/hpp-progress-to-date. The "proteome" refers to all human proteins, estimated to range from hundreds of thousands to millions. This number is much greater than the number of protein-coding genes. Additional proteins are made in two ways. One is "alternative splicing." Instead of using all the DNA code from a protein-coding gene, different sections are spliced together to code for another protein. (This received the 1993 Nobel Prize in Physiology or Medicine.) The other is called "post-translational modifications." Proteins produced by ribosomes are chemically modified to become new proteins.

If you have not had the chance to watch Dr. Georgia Purdom's presentation, "Wonder of DNA," watch it now. In it, she explains how evolutionary biologists resist accepting new research that shows "junk DNA" is not junk. This resistance is an example of confirmation bias. Re-titled "Evolutionists Hate When You Bring This Up," this video is on the YouTube channel "Answers in Genesis."

For those interested in the mathematical probability of chance development of proteins, watch a video titled "What is the probability of a functional protein existing by chance?" It shows Dr. Stephen Meyer teaching a class of university students. Find this video on the YouTube channel "Test of Believers."

Chapter 13

How can I read Darwin's book to judge for myself?

Darwin's *On the Origin of Species* is challenging to read because it is long and has many observations of nature. An alternative is to read an adapted version called *On the Origin of Species: Young Readers Edition* by Rebecca Stefoff (Atheneum Books for Young Readers, 2018). The publisher says it is meticulously curated to honor Darwin's original text. However, it is essential to stay skeptical while reading this book. Then, you can avoid being influenced by apophenia as Darwin was.

It is also important to consider three critical issues while reading his book.

The first issue is that Darwin's book drowns its readers. The book discusses many aspects of nature, and he engages in lengthy discussions. Maintaining a critical mind while reading a long argument spanning five hundred pages is difficult, if not impossible. Readers can become so tired that they will accept the book's conclusions out of exhaustion.

The particular problem is this. Darwin's many observations of nature focus on "breeding" or changes within a species. For instance, he will discuss slight changes in the length and shape of a bird's beak to adapt to a different type of food. His observations do not include how an existing species becomes a new species with distinct body parts.

As you read Darwin's descriptions of nature, you must ask yourself: Is he describing minor changes from breeding within a species? Or is he describing the development of new species having new anatomical structures? This distinction is crucial. Minor changes within a species do not serve as examples of the evolution of new species.

If Darwin only describes breeding "within a species," such as in dogs, he is not showing how dogs transform into another kind of animal.

The second issue is that Darwin formed his conclusions from limited information. In his book, Darwin explained his theory's difficulties with complex organs when he wrote:

> To suppose that the eye, with all its inimitable contrivances for adjusting the focus to different distances, for admitting different amounts of light, and for the correction of spherical and chromatic aberration, could have been formed by natural selection, seems, I freely confess, absurd in the highest possible degree.
>
> Origin of Species 1859 edition, p. 186

Yet Darwin then stated that natural selection could explain the origin of the human eye!

It is worth bearing in mind that in 1859 when Darwin published his book, he only understood the front of the eye—the iris, the lens, and how the eye focuses light. He was unaware of the incredible complexity of the back of the eye. He could not see the retina's 100+ million photoreceptors that convert photons of light into electrical signals for the brain.

Only in the last few decades have scientists discovered that the retina does not simply send a raw image to the brain's visual cortex, as most people believe. Dr. Richard Masland, the former Distinguished David G. Cogan Professor of Ophthalmology and Professor of Neurobiology at Harvard Medical School, is the leading authority on eye research. He writes, "The retina is a microprocessor, like the one contained in your cellphone, your camera, or your wristwatch." (*We Know It When We See It.* Richard Masland, Basic Books, 2020, p.19)

In the retina, nerve cells do not only receive the image. They also *enhance* the image. Dr. Masland describes special neurons—a type of information-transmitting nerve cell—that detect the edges of objects in the image. Other neurons detect specific movement directions—left, right, up, or down—for each point in the visual image. This enhancement of visual elements emphasizes important movements and actions for the brain. At the same time, it de-emphasizes areas with no changes, like the middle of the sky or solid color surfaces.

Retinal image processing involves more than just edge detection and movement direction. Approximately 30 different streams of information about each point of the image are simultaneously transmitted to the brain.

Retinal image processing has many benefits. For instance, by detecting the movement and direction of an object promptly, we can react faster, like dodging a basketball flying towards us. It also helps stabilize the images we see, preventing them from bouncing as we walk or jog.

Professor Masland states, "...Darwin did not know the structure of the retina: if he had, his slowly gestating treatise on evolution might never have been published." ("The Neuronal Organization of the Retina." Richard H. Masland. Neuron, Volume 76, Issue 2, pp. 266-280, October 18, 2012.)

The third issue is one that Dr. Michael Behe identifies in his book *Darwin Devolves*. Darwin never showed that natural selection can build complex organs and structures. Instead, he only proposes that they might. One could further say that Darwin's idea that natural selection can create complex organs is pure conjecture. As explained in the discussion of molecular machines, we now know that some structures are irreducibly complex. They cannot possibly have evolved gradually over millions of years, as Darwin suggested.

Finally, in the Introduction to his book, *Origin of Species*, Darwin writes:

> For I am well aware that scarcely a single point is discussed in this volume on which facts cannot be adduced, often apparently leading to conclusions directly opposite to those at which I have arrived. A fair result can be obtained only by fully stating and balancing the facts and arguments on both sides of each question; and this cannot possibly be here done.
>
> Origin of Species, 1859 edition, p.10

This quote shows Darwin's book is one long argument for his theory. He admits it is not a balanced presentation of facts, and it is impossible to arrive at a reasonable conclusion based on reading it!

If you read Darwin's book, recognize that it is a one-sided interpretation of data specifically chosen to make his case. To judge his theory properly, you must look for and consider counterarguments yourself.

Throughout his life, Charles Darwin forcefully argued for his theory of evolution. Like other evolutionary biologists, public assertions carry a tone of certainty. Yet, in private communications, a different tone emerges. On April 3, 1860, Darwin wrote a letter to Asa Gray, an American botanist who supported evolutionary theory. Darwin revealed his discomfort with what he saw:

> I remember well time when the thought of the eye made me cold all over, but I have got over this stage of the complaint, & now small trifling particulars of structure often make me very uncomfortable. The sight of a feather in a peacock's tail, whenever I gaze at it, makes me sick!
>
> April 3, 1860 letter to Asa Gray

You can read the letter by visiting the University of Cambridge's Darwin Correspondence Project website: "darwinproject.ac.uk." Search for the term "small trifling particulars of structure."

The peacock feather has a unique pattern and complex structure. Darwin could see evidence of complexity that he knew could not be explained by evolution. When faced with evidence that challenges his theory, Darwin becomes distressed. The conflict between his beliefs and the evidence before him is too great for him to ignore.

Darwin's reaction is an example of *cognitive dissonance*. This term refers to a psychological state identified by Dr. Leon Festinger in 1957. The term describes the psychological discomfort people feel when they have conflicting beliefs, attitudes, or values. They also feel this discomfort when encountering information that contradicts their beliefs. This discomfort can create emotional distress and make a person feel "sick."

Given that Darwin and other evolutionary biologists harbor private doubts about evolutionary theory, we should approach their public statements cautiously. We should not be misled by what they say for public consumption. We need to assess the evidence for ourselves.

Watch this excellent presentation by Dr. Stuart Burgess titled "Hallmarks of Design–Professor Stuart Burgess." He explains why seeing a peacock's tail feather would make Charles Darwin feel sick. He explains that the tail feathers' colors are not organic pigments. Instead, prism-like structures reflecting light, called "thin-film interference," produce iridescent colors.* The peacock needs significant amounts of biological information to make its beautiful patterns from the prism-like structures. You can find this video on the YouTube channel "Stephen Carter."

*Note. If Charles Darwin had felt sick when gazing at a peacock's tail feather, he would have also felt uncomfortable looking at other beautiful creatures. These include butterflies, peacock spiders, the jewel beetle, the rainbow boa snake, and the Siamese fighting fish. These and other living creatures create beautiful, iridescent, structural colors through thin film interference.

Chapter 14

Isn't evolution part of science and therefore fact?

Science Changes Through the Ages

Evolutionary theory is widely accepted in science. We trust science because we see how science improves our daily lives. We use cell phones and take medicines doctors prescribe. We use them even though we do not understand how they work. Indeed, we accept new technologies and medicine on faith. We do not investigate every scientific detail ourselves. It is impractical, even if we could understand the science.

The same goes for the theory of evolution. Most people accept the theory of evolution because they trust science. Indeed, scientists outside of biology accept it in the same way non-scientists do. They trust science and accept the theory without studying it themselves. They rely on what they hear about evolution through the media we consume.

Recognizing that what is considered a scientific fact can change over time is important. Until the mid-1800s, scientists and the public believed life could emerge from non-living matter. This concept was known as "spontaneous generation." People believed fleas came from dust and maggots from decaying flesh. The idea that insects could emerge without parents is far-fetched today. But it was accepted when Charles Darwin lived.

But, something important happened after Darwin published his Origin of Species in 1859. The French scientist Louis Pasteur conducted experiments that disproved spontaneous generation.

He did a critical set of experiments. Pasteur sterilized a nutrient broth so that there would be no living organisms in the broth. He placed some of this broth in a flask designed to prevent contamination. He also put some in another flask that allowed exposure to outside air.

The results were revealing. The broth exposed to the outside air showed the growth of microorganisms. In contrast, the broth in the contamination-proof flask had no microorganisms. His experiment proved that microorganisms in the air caused contamination. This experiment disproved the theory of spontaneous generation.

The scientific community did not immediately abandon the theory of spontaneous generation. Despite Pasteur's experiments, many scientists persevered in their beliefs. They continued to believe life could emerge without parents! After further experiments and evidence from other scientists, the scientific community changed. They finally agreed that spontaneous generation was impossible. Thus, after an accumulation of evidence, the theory of spontaneous generation was discarded. The new theory of *biogenesis* replaced it. This term describes the new scientific finding that "life comes from life."

Louis Pasteur is one of the most remarkable scientists in history. Scientists consider him to be the "father of bacteriology." His experiments proved germs caused diseases. He pioneered pasteurization by proving that heating milk eradicated microorganisms. He also developed vaccines using weakened microbes. Pasteur's discoveries have saved millions of lives throughout history.

The change from spontaneous generation to biogenesis shows how science changes. Dr. Thomas Kuhn explains how scientific thought develops in stages. In his book, *The Structure of Scientific Revolutions* (University of Chicago Press, 2012), he describes a *paradigm shift*. This term refers to how science moves to a new theory and accepted methods. It is a process that takes several steps.

Initially, a scientific field of study grows. Scientists agree on its concepts and methods. There is a time of normal science. Normal science is a period where scientists routinely work within the established theories. But over time, unexpected discoveries appear. These discoveries do not fit the expected pattern. During this phase, scientists ignore findings that do not fit their theories. They may even suppress the new information. That is because the new evidence threatens to undermine their established views.

However, at some point, there are too many serious inconsistencies. Scientists can no longer ignore the new facts. So, a crisis develops. When the old guard can no longer defend their cherished theories, a new theory takes hold. The scientific consensus changes.[1]

So, although evolution is now considered mainstream science, we can see it differently. We can see that evolution is part of Kuhn's "normal science" stage. In this stage, scientists ignore and suppress conflicting evidence. They dismiss alternative views.

---

1. A notable example of a change in the scientific consensus is the acceptance that the universe had a beginning. Up until the 1960s, most scientists thought that the universe was static. They thought it always existed, contrary to the Bible, which said there was a beginning. However, measurements soon showed that the universe had a beginning. Eventually, scientists reached a new consensus consistent with the Book of Genesis.

So, scientists can be expected to dismiss views that conflict with their evolutionary theories. They, therefore, dismiss the improbability of DNA's instructional codes occurring by chance. They reject the existence of irreducible complexity. Nothing is considered too complex for the evolutionary process. Even molecular machines can arise by evolution. And they ignore evidence that mutations can only produce minor changes, not new animal species.

Looking back, Darwin's theory of evolution has been around since 1859. It has had over 160 years to become accepted as mainstream science. Yet, it was only in 2022 that scientists finally decoded the last eight percent of the human genome! Only in the past 25 years have scientists come to understand how our cells' molecular machines create all the tissues in our body!

With this new understanding of DNA and molecular machines, biology is changing. Biologists who have spent their entire lives viewing life as only matter and energy are being challenged. The information processing in the cell is moving biology towards a new paradigm. As people understand the implications of these discoveries, foundations for evolutionary theory will crumble.

If Darwin Lived Today

The scientific community strongly supports the theory of evolution. However, affected by apophenia, evolutionary scientists only see evidence that confirms their beliefs. They cannot allow themselves to consider alternative perspectives.

If Charles Darwin were alive today, he could say he had valid reasons for his beliefs. When he wrote *Origin of Species*, the field of cell biology did not exist. But since then, science has progressed. In the 20th century, electron microscopes allowed us to see inside cells. X-ray crystallography allowed scientists to understand DNA and molecular machines. The new cell and molecular biology fields have advanced significantly with these developments. Today, scientists can create stunning animations. They can do this thanks to powerful computers used in video games. These animations help us see how DNA and molecular machines work inside the cell.

If Darwin were alive today, he would witness the incredible molecular machine, *Topoisomerase*. What is Topoisomerase? (pronounced as "toh-poh-ai-saw-mr-aise")

Dr. James C. Wang, Harvard University's Mallinckrodt Professor of Biochemistry and Molecular Biology, discovered Topoisomerase enzymes. He calls them the "magicians of the DNA world."

The DNA is a double helix comprising two strands that twist. Unwound, they would stretch out six feet. However, inside the cell's nucleus, DNA is tightly coiled and packed. But what happens during replication when the two coiled and twisted strands must be pulled apart? The strands become a tangled mess!

So, how do cells fix the tangled strands? The Topoisomerase molecular machine goes to each tangle and cuts the DNA strand. These cuts allow the DNA strand to straighten. Then, the Topoisomerase enzyme re-joins the two cut pieces!

If Darwin could have seen Topoisomerase in action, perhaps he would no longer believe that life only seems designed. Instead, he might say molecular machines, like Topoisomerase, were brilliantly designed by our Creator.

You can read the story of how Dr. James Wang accidentally discovered Topoisomerase, as told in his Harvard University biography. This biography is at the webpage: https://www.mcb.harvard.edu/directory/james-wang/

Watch the video called "Untangler of Knots: The Amazing Topoisomerase Molecular Machine." You can find this video on the YouTube channel "Discovery Science."

But blessed are your eyes, for they see, and your ears,
for they hear. For truly, I say to you, many prophets and righteous
people longed to see what you see, and did not see it,
and to hear what you hear, and did not hear it.

Matthew 13:16-17

Chapter 15

"How life began" and the story of the clever alien

Although there are many ideas of how life began, science educators teach students the *primordial soup theory*. According to this theory, when Earth was young, chemicals in the oceans self-assembled into simple living cells. Life, therefore, came from non-life! Does this idea sound familiar?

Textbooks teach the primordial soup theory complementing Darwin's theory of how animals and plants evolved. As Darwin's book is about the origin of species and all species were supposed to have descended from a common ancestor, what was the common ancestor? Evolutionary biologists say there must have been a first single-cell ancestor to all life. They call this cell *LUCA*. This is an acronym for "Last Universal Common Ancestor," a term invented in the 1990s.

The term "Last Universal Common Ancestor" is confusing. Why is the first cell, supposedly the ancestor of all life, called "Last?"

Evolutionary scientists theorize that billions of years ago, there were many single-celled organisms. They theorize that they all died except for one. That organism would be the last survivor. That last cell supposedly began Darwin's evolutionary journey. But, while evolutionary biologists believe that LUCA must have existed, this is hypothetical. Naturally, no one has seen this cell.

The primordial soup theory supposedly answers the question of how the first cells appeared.

Biology textbooks often describe the Miller-Urey experiment. They use it to support the idea that life arose from a primordial soup. In 1952, a chemist named Dr. Harold Urey worked with his graduate student, Stanley Miller. Together, they conducted their famous experiment. They assembled a glass apparatus containing only four ingredients. These were methane, ammonia, hydrogen, and water. They excluded oxygen because they assumed early Earth had no oxygen. The apparatus heated the water. It also circulated the gases past a high-voltage spark to simulate lightning. After a week, the experiment produced dark red, turbid water. When they analyzed this dark water, they found small amounts of several amino acids. As some of these amino acids are known to be required for making proteins, scientists celebrated this result. The science community was jubilant. They considered this a demonstration that the primordial soup could have created the building blocks of life.

Unfortunately, evolutionary scientists could not produce further advances in the following 70 years. A chemical reaction that formed a few rudimentary molecules required for life is far from creating life. No one could turn the amino acids into proteins, the building blocks of body tissues.[1]

Today, evolutionary scientists still do not know how life formed. Yet they are sure that life came from non-living matter

---

1. Miller and Urey conducted their experiment in 1952. This experiment was conducted before Watson & Crick's 1953 discovery of DNA's structure and other Nobel Prize-winning scientists' discoveries, which showed how molecular machines read DNA's genetic code to make proteins.

through chemical reactions. Textbooks continue to describe the Miller-Urey experiment. They suggest this is evidence for the primordial soup theory.

Incredibly, there has never been an example of life coming from non-life. Yet many intelligent scientists believe that life originated in such a way. They believe simple chemicals can assemble themselves. They can "evolve" into proteins and other needed cell components such as DNA, lipid membranes,[2] and carbohydrates. Evolutionary scientists call this early process "chemical evolution." This term is misleading as chemicals do not evolve—chemicals react.

Abiogenesis is the name used for the theory that, billions of years ago, simple chemicals assembled into living cells on their own. One of Darwin's greatest early supporters, Thomas Huxley, coined the term. But he did not believe in abiogenesis. He introduced the term to contrast it with *biogenesis*, the now-accepted scientific theory that life comes from life.

Why do intelligent people believe in abiogenesis? One explanation is that people cannot see what happens at a molecular level. Another is that few people have taken university-level organic chemistry courses. They do not understand organic chemistry and cannot visualize chemical processes. As a result, people cannot apply common sense to judge what is being taught. So, let us consider a story to help understand what evolutionary scientists teach.

Let us imagine again that aliens have come to Earth. Human beings have long been gone. The aliens find modern houses everywhere. They have walls, windows, and electric appliances. The alien scientists try to understand their origin. After much

---

2. The lipid membrane is a flexible barrier around the cell. It is selectively permeable allowing only certain nutrients, molecules and ions to pass into and out of the cell.

thought, a clever alien proposes a theory to explain the emergence of houses.

The clever alien's theory says that billions of years ago, early Earth comprised oceans and rocky land. During this period, massive meteorites crashed into the rocky terrain. The tremendous energy generated by the impact caused extensive melting of the rocks. Minerals and ores became molten, producing small amounts of pure iron and copper. The quartz in the rocks melted and then cooled, transforming into glass.

The alien scientist says: "The crushed rock, along with the pure iron, copper, and glass, must have been the building blocks of houses!"

He continues, "The crushed rocks formed themselves into bricks, which then arranged themselves into walls. Because of gravity, the glass flattened into sheets that later became windows. Meanwhile, the iron formed itself into pipes, and copper naturally extended itself into wire."

The alien scientist explains, "Certain rocks possessed magnetic properties and transformed into magnets. Through a self-assembly process, the copper wire, iron pipes, and magnets came together to form generators. The iron pipes brought water from the river to the generator, creating electricity. Simultaneously, glass and metal self-organized into lightbulbs and kitchen appliances. The copper wire connected the generator to the houses' lights and appliances."

The alien scientist happily shouts, "Aha! Fully functioning houses with electricity! I will call this the 'primordial rock theory!'"

Now, using our common sense, we see the absurdity of this primordial rock theory. The idea of meteorites colliding into rocks to form houses is absurd. Similarly, the theory of basic chemicals combining themselves into living cells is absurd.

This is a perfect time for the boy in the story of "The Emperor's New Clothes" to shout, "The Emperor has no clothes!" If only we had an authoritative scientist in organic chemistry who would come to our rescue. He could shout, "These theories of chemical evolution are nonsense!" Only an expert organic chemist can authoritatively refute scientists who claim that life evolved from non-living matter in warm puddles* or deep-sea hydrothermal vents.

~ℓℓ~

*Charles Darwin's *Origin of Species* did not discuss how life began. However, 12 years later, in 1871, he wrote a letter to Joseph Hooker. In it, Darwin wrote, "...we could conceive in some warm pond with all sorts of ammonia & phosphoric salts,—light, heat, electricity etc. present, that a protein compound was chemically formed, ready to undergo still more complex changes...." So Darwin thought, or at least speculated, that life originated through abiogenesis, essentially the primordial soup theory. You can read the letter containing this quote. Go to the University of Cambridge's Darwin Correspondence Project website: "darwinproject.ac.uk" and enter the search term "warm pond."

~ℓℓ~

Fortunately, a leading scientist is exposing the folly of origin-of-life research scientists. His name is Dr. James M. Tour. He is the T.T. and W.F. Chao Professor of Chemistry and Professor of Materials Science & Nanoengineering at Rice University. He is one of the few synthetic organic chemists[3] worldwide whose expertise is making molecules and nanotechnology. In 2013, R&D Magazine named Dr. Tour "Scientist of the Year."

---

3. A synthetic organic chemist specializes in synthesizing or creating organic compounds through chemical reactions.

As one of the world's leading experts in synthetic organic chemistry, Dr. James Tour is now teaching the public why the primordial soup theory is nonsense. You can find his videos on his YouTube channel called "DrJamesTour."

One of his talks at Andrews University is titled "Scientists are Clueless on the Origin of Life." It is an excellent video for several reasons. He explains why abiogenesis is nonsense based on how chemistry works. He also explains the enormous challenges in creating the complex structures of living cells.

On top of that, he bravely speaks the truth. He exposes the misleading aspects of "origin-of-life research" conducted by evolutionary scientists. He also exposes false claims published in respected scientific journals.

> Watch Dr. Tour's lecture at Andrews University called "Scientists are Clueless on the Origin of Life." Most people will not understand every point presented. However, it is still highly worthwhile to watch. You can find this video on the YouTube channel "Dr. James Tour."

For those who do not have time to watch Dr. Tour's videos, here is a simple explanation why basic chemicals alone cannot create life: Chemical reactions do not produce the genetic information essential for life.

Even if we could assemble DNA or RNA molecules[4] with chemical reactions, they would not have any genetic information. Think of DNA or mRNA like a computer's flash drive or

---

4. While DNA is double-stranded, RNA is single-stranded. RNA is more transient and can form secondary structures to serve multiple roles, including mRNA.

thumb drive used to store or transfer computer files. There is no information in the drive until you put data files on it.

Origin-of-life scientists and the media enjoy discussing how life might have started from a primordial soup. But, they cannot explain where the genetic information in the cell's DNA or RNA comes from. They also cannot explain where molecular machines come from. Without molecular machines, cells cannot divide, and cells would not make proteins. Early cells could never grow or reproduce.

Chapter 16

Does Bill Gates really think it is reasonable to believe in God?

The March 13, 2014 edition of Rolling Stones featured an article called "Bill Gates: The Rolling Stones Interview." When asked if he believes in God, Bill Gates explains. He states, "...the mystery and the beauty of the world is overwhelmingly amazing, and there's no scientific explanation of how it came about. To say that it was generated by random numbers, that does seem, you know, sort of an uncharitable view [laughs]. I think it makes sense to believe in God...."

In essence, Bill Gates' statement implies that the theory of evolution based on random chance is not a reasonable explanation. In contrast, believing in God as the Creator of our universe makes more sense.

When talking about the mystery and the beauty of the world, one of the most captivating and mysterious is the immense variety of birds on our planet. They intrigue and delight us. They have unique shapes and sizes. They come in beautiful colors. And how they build their nests and feed their chicks can be fascinating. But above all else, we admire how they can fly.

Birds have the gift of flight. The gradual process of "survival of the fittest" cannot explain the development of flight. Dr. Stuart Burgess, Professor of Engineering Design at the University of Bristol, explains why. He says that the design of birds is an example of an irreducibly complex system. Birds need many simultaneous design innovations for flight.

He explains that the bird's wingbone mechanism is unique. It allows the elbow muscles to move the wrist joints automatically. The wing is lighter and more efficient as it needs little muscle at the wrist joint. This design also enables birds to fold their wings easily. Being structurally light in weight is critical to flight.

Wing design and other features, such as the tail, which controls the direction of flight, must come together simultaneously. Birds with wings but no tails cannot fly.

Birds cannot simply evolve the anatomical parts needed to fly in a step-by-step process. It is like the saying, "You can't be half-pregnant." Flight requires many components in an "all or nothing" manner. The various components must arrive simultaneously.

Dr. Burgess explains that the Wright brothers faced a similar problem. It happened when they were making the first airplane. With wings alone, their aircraft could not fly. After observing how pigeons used their tails to control flight, the Wright brothers added a tail to their airplane. They found that they needed several innovations simultaneously before their plane could fly. The brothers' airplane required aerodynamic wings, lightweight structures, and control mechanisms. Only then could they produce their famous first airplane flight in Kitty Hawk, North Carolina.

> Watch this video titled "In What Ways Did God Design Animals and People? - Dr. Stuart Burgess" to see how Dr. Burgess explains the irreducible complexity of flight. Find this video on the YouTube channel "Is Genesis History?"

Dr. Andrew McIntosh holds a Ph.D. in Aeronautics. He is a professional engineer and a Professor of Thermodynamics and Combustion Theory at the University of Leeds. He explains other bird features that could not have evolved gradually through natural selection because they are irreducibly complex.

One such feature is the intricate composition of their wings:

1. Large primary flight feathers are on the outer part of wings. They bear the greatest aerodynamic load. These feathers are crucial for flight.

2. Secondary feathers maintain stability.

3. Covert feathers cover the base of the flight feathers. These thicken the wing's leading edge to create an aerofoil shape.

Each feather is also more intricate than meets the eye. A bird's feather has a central stem known as the rachis. It serves as the central axis of the feather. Growing outward from the rachis on each side are branches called *barbs*. Barbs comprise the vane that you see next to the central stem. But if the barbs grow outward from the rachis, how do all the barbs connect to form a flat, smooth surface?

The answer can only be seen with a microscope. The barbs have tiny velcro-like appendages that lock the barbs together. These appendages are called barbules. But the system is much better than velcro. Velcro is a system of hooks and loops.

Unlike velcro, barbules have hooks and ridges. On one side, they have hooks, while on the other, they have ridges. This design lets the hooks grip the ridges while letting them slide to different positions along the ridges.

The design of this sliding system, with its microscopic hooks and ridges, is ingenious. It allows for positioning adjustments. During a wing's downstroke, the hooks and ridges can tightly lock the barbs together, preventing air from seeping through the feathers. However, this positioning changes on the upstroke, creating gaps that allow air to pass through the wing's feathers. This system maximizes the energy efficiency of the flapping wing.

So, the next time you pick up a feather and pull the vane apart, you will know why you cannot join it together again. The microscopic hooks have been unhooked from the ridges.

Have you ever wondered how birds can fly great distances? They continuously flap their wings without stopping to rest. Humans run short distances and need to stop to catch their breath. Dr. McIntosh explains that birds have a remarkable respiratory system. It differs from mammals and reptiles. In humans, tiny sacs in our lungs called alveoli inflate and deflate as we inhale and exhale. In contrast, birds have respiratory systems that allow oxygen to flow through their lungs continuously without inflating alveoli.

Their breathing system is so efficient that they do not need a diaphragm to pump air in and out of their lungs. The muscles that make the wings flap run across the sternum or breastbone. As the muscles power the wings, they push the sternum. This moves the air through their respiratory system.

The features needed for flight are incredible, from birds' feathers to their respiratory system. Dr. McIntosh states that these components are irreducibly complex systems. The parts of each system must come together at the same time. They could not have evolved through natural selection. The features of bird flight are evidence of design.

> Read Dr. McIntosh's paper titled "Evidence of Design in Bird Feathers and Avian Respiration" to learn more about feathers and how birds breathe. It is published in the *International Journal of Design & Nature and Ecodynamics,* Vol. 4, No. 2 (2009), pp. 154-169. To read the full paper, visit www.witpress and enter "Avian Respiration" in the search.

Of all living things, God has a particular commandment on how we should treat birds. The Book of Deuteronomy 22:6-7 states:

> If you come across a bird's nest in any tree or on the ground, with young ones or eggs and the mother sitting on the young or on the eggs, you shall not take the mother with the young. You shall let the mother go, but the young you may take for yourself, that it may go well with you, and that you may live long.

In God's created order, it is normal for raccoons to climb trees to eat bird eggs, and crows or eagles to raid a nest to eat eggs or baby birds. In these instances, the mother survives, enabling her to create a new nest and produce more offspring.

If humans take the mother along with her young or her eggs, through their greed, they will destroy a valuable resource. Allowing the mother to escape and reproduce ensures the health and balance of the ecosystem.

The maintenance of our ecosystem and the resources it provides is why the instruction promises that if you follow this direction, it will "go well with you, and that you may live long." In his book, *The Rational Bible: Deuteronomy* (Regnery Faith, 2022), Dennis Prager notes that this is one of only three commandments accompanied by the promise of a long life. The first one is the commandment to honor your parents, found in Exodus 20:12. The last one is the commandment to act honestly in business, found in Deuteronomy 25:15. We can now see that protecting our ecosystem is as important as honoring our parents and being honest in business.

Individuals who do not honor their parents lose their parents' guidance and support. Their parents can even disinherit them, resulting in loss of property and family connections. Individuals who are dishonest in business can suffer retribution from those they cheat. The consequences of disobeying either of these commandments can be life-altering.

Another aspect of this instruction to allow the mother bird to fly away is that God is very protective of his created order. As mentioned previously, Leviticus 19:19 states, "You shall keep my statutes. You shall not let your cattle breed with a different kind." Protecting the mother bird's ability to have more offspring and not letting cattle breed with a different kind both have the same effect. They both ensure the healthy continuation of the natural world as God created it.

Chapter 17

"The Emperor's New Clothes" and searching for truth

C. A. Reitzel published "The Emperor's New Clothes" in Copenhagen on April 7, 1837. As an early story of political correctness when only a child will speak the truth, it is worth reading whether reading it for the first time or revisiting it.

> Read "The Emperor's New Clothes," a translation of Hans Christian Andersen's "Keiserens Nye Klæder" by Jean Hersholt. Find it by entering "The Emperor's New Clothes Translation" into a Google search.

As important as speaking the truth, it is equally important to search for it properly. In 2010, the science magazine *Discover* published an article titled "Why Scientific Studies Are So Often Wrong: The Streetlight Effect." In this article, David Freedman explains that scientists often make a fundamental mistake. To illustrate this mistake, he tells an old story called "The Streetlight Parable" or "The Drunkard's Search":

> Late at night, a police officer finds a drunk man crawling around on his hands and knees under a streetlight. The drunk man tells the officer he's looking for his wallet. When the officer asks if he's sure this is where he dropped the wallet, the man replies that he thinks he more likely dropped it across the street. "Then why are you looking over here?" the befuddled officer asks. "Because the light's better here," explains the drunk man.

Freedman uses this parable to illustrate that scientists often make a crucial error. They focus their search only on where the light is better rather than where the truth is more likely. Researchers know this error as the streetlight effect.

The streetlight effect is a critical mistake that impacts evolutionary biologists. We see it when evolutionary biologists respond to Dr. Stephen Meyer. Dr Meyer writes that DNA's complex code points to an intelligent source that created the code. But, evolutionary biologists claim that such a conclusion is "unscientific." They argue that his conclusion goes outside the bounds of science. This argument implies that science can only deal with physical processes or the material world. It is clear that such biologists are only searching for what is "under the streetlight."

Depending solely on science for explanations is an example of "the streetlight effect." Dr. John Lennox, Professor of Mathematics at Oxford University (Emeritus), explains the error of relying only on scientific explanations. In his book, *Can Science Explain Everything?* (The Good Book Company, 2019),

Dr. Lennox explains that there are two types of explanations. He writes:

> Suppose you ask: *Why is this water boiling?* I may say that the heat energy from the gas flame is being conducted through the copper base of the kettle and is agitating the molecules of the water to such an extent that the water is boiling.
>
> Or I may say that the water is boiling because I would like a cup of tea.

Dr. Lennox explains that both answers are equally rational. The first explanation, based on the conduction of heat energy, is scientific. The second explanation, based on a person wanting to drink some tea, involves a person's intention. Someone's mind desires a purposeful outcome. Moreover, depending on the question, a full explanation requires both types of answers. In many cases, personal intention is more important than the scientific answer.

Dr Lennox once discussed God and why we are here with students at Brown University. In this discussion, Dr. Lennox said his child once asked him, "Why am I here, daddy?"

Dr. Lennox answered them, "Because I wanted you to be."

He explained to the students, "God wanted you to be," and "Someone wanting you is a wonderful thing in life." This explanation differs from the scientific answer that usually comes to mind—a child is here because a father's sperm cell fertilized a mother's egg cell.

Dr. Lennox's perspective on the nature of explanation is crucial. When scientists only look for a "scientific" answer and ignore possible reasons that involve an intention or purpose, their search for the truth is compromised.

Accordingly, scientists should consider Dr. Meyer's conclusion. An intelligent source as an explanation for DNA's sophisticated code is a perfectly rational inference. Scientists must look beyond the streetlight, which shines only on their study of physical processes and the material world.

> Watch Dr. John Lennox's talk titled "Why Are We Here? God, Life, and the Pursuit of Happiness | John Lennox at Brown." You can find this video on the YouTube channel "The Veritas Forum."

Another aspect of "looking under the streetlight" involves scientists failing to consider engineering design principles. Evolutionary biologists claim that the natural world only *appears* to be designed. Yet, as Dr. Stuart Burgess states, evolutionary biologists fail to investigate whether living organisms exhibit optimal design. They also neglect to examine if the organs and structures of living creatures are irreducibly complex.

Theodore Von Karman, an aerospace engineer, is considered the "father of supersonic flight." He received the first U.S. National Medal of Science award in 1962. As featured on the U.S. National Science Foundation webpage describing his life's work, he once said:

> Scientists study the world as it is, engineers create the world that never has been.

This quotation highlights the difference between scientists and engineers—scientists study, but engineers create. When evolutionary scientists neglect to view the world from the perspective of engineers who design and create, they miss the clear evidence of God's creation.

These scientists resemble the blind men in the ancient fable of the six blind men and the elephant. One feels the trunk and says the animal is like a snake. Another touches the ear and says it is like a fan. Another feels the leg and says it is like a tree trunk. Yet another person handling the tusk says it is like a smooth spear. A man touching the elephant's side says it resembles a wall. And a man touching the tail says it is like a rope. Each man is partly right and partly wrong. If only they could see all the parts of the elephant together.

When the evolutionary paleontologist points to a fossilized fish fin and says it is like a human hand, he acts just like the blind men in this story!

Scientists must approach the study of life from the perspective of how a whole animal is engineered. This perspective will let them to see the natural world as it truly is. Then, they will see the creative genius of God.

Watch Dr. Stuart Burgess present "Why Human Skeletal Joints are Masterpieces of Engineering." As an engineering professor, Dr. Burgess demonstrates how an evolutionary scientist can be incredibly wrong because he does not understand engineering. This highly recommended video can be found on the YouTube "Discovery Science" channel.

Read Dr. Andrew McIntosh's excellent article "The Intricacies of Flight in the Natural World." Drawing on his expertise as an aeronautical engineer, Dr. McIntosh provides a perspective that allows you to appreciate the true essence of the natural world. Find it by entering "The Intricacies of Flight in the Natural World" in a Google search.

"And God Blessed Them"

For the Lord is good;
his steadfast love endures forever,
and his faithfulness to all generations.

Psalm 100:5

Introduction

We are not only created by God but are continually blessed by Him in countless ways. Many people may not fully appreciate the extent of these blessings, which include our healthcare, educational system, and freedom from slavery. This section highlights these gifts and the unique abilities bestowed upon us as human beings.

Chapter 18

How did the birth of Jesus result in hospitals?

In ancient Roman times, facilities to care for the sick or wounded were provided only to soldiers, gladiators, and certain slaves. The general population had no access. People who were ill were left to die. Those with leprosy were driven out of the town. However, the Bible records that Jesus traveled the countryside. He miraculously healed illnesses and diseases, including those with leprosy. He also instructed his disciples to go out "to proclaim the kingdom of God and to *heal*" (Luke 9:2).

Jesus' love and compassion inspired a new attitude toward those who were ill. His followers, called Christians, became known as those who had compassion for sick people. Christians believed that by serving those who were ill, they were serving God and doing as Jesus commanded.

Christianity placed a high value on caring for the sick, and Christians formally put this value into practice. In 325 AD, Christian leaders held the first World Church Council in Nicaea, Turkey. At this meeting, the leaders decreed that there should be a hospital wherever there was a church. This directive has had a lasting impact through the centuries; many hospitals still bear Christian names. They include names such as Holy Cross

Hospital, Baptist Hospital, St. Joseph's Hospital, Grace Hospital, etc. Hospitals were Christian institutions!

The practice of nursing, an essential aspect of hospital care, also has its origins in Christianity. Driven by their dedication to Jesus, women would join convents where they devoted themselves to caring for the hospital's patients. These early caregivers were the forerunners of modern nurses.

You can read more in the excellent book *What If Jesus Had Never Been Born* (D. James Kennedy & Jerry Newcomb, Nelson Books, 2001).

***

And great crowds came to him, bringing with them
the lame, the blind, the crippled, the mute, and many others,
and they put them at his feet, and he healed them.

Matthew 15:30

Chapter 19

Why did universities arise from Christianity?

The establishment of universities can be traced to the desire to teach the Christian faith. In his book, *How Christianity Changed the World* (Zondervan, 2004), Alvin J. Schmitt explains. Schmitt writes that by the time of the US Civil War, Christian denominations had founded 92% of the 182 colleges and universities in the United States.

Indeed, many of the most prominent universities in the United States have their roots in Christian denominations. Some examples are:

- Harvard College (that became Harvard University) was established in 1635 by the Congregational Church as a theological institution. Harvard University's motto, adopted in 1692, was "Veritas Christo et Ecclesiae." It is Latin for "Truth for the Church and Christ."

- Yale University mainly began as a Congregational institution to educate ministers.

- Northwestern University was founded by the Methodists.

- Columbia University, originally King's College, was Episcopalian. Its motto is "In Lumine Tuo Videbimis Lumen." It is the Latin translation of Psalm 36:9 in the Bible, which says, "In your light, we see the light."

- Princeton University began as a Presbyterian school. Its motto is "Dei Sub Numine Viget," Latin for "Under God's Power She Flourishes."

- Brown University was started by Baptists. Its motto is "In Deo Speramus," which is Latin for "In God We Trust." (This English phrase appeared on US coins beginning in 1864. It also became the national motto of the United States in 1956.)

The origins and mottos of these institutions provide insight into the significant influence of Christianity on early American education and our moral values.

In neighboring Canada, the University of Laval is the country's oldest university. It is an offshoot of the Seminary of Quebec, a society of diocesan priests founded in 1663. University of Laval's motto is "Deo favente haud pluribus impar." It is Latin for "By the grace of God, to no one equal."

One of the leading universities in Canada is Queen's University. It was established as Queen's College in 1841 by the Church of Scotland. Queen's first classes in 1842 prepared students for ministry. Queen's University's motto is "Sapientia et Doctrina Stabilitas." It means, "Wisdom and knowledge shall be the stability of thy times." This motto was adapted from Isaiah 33:6.

Alvin Schmitt's book, *How Christianity Changed the World*, explains that most European universities, such as Oxford, Paris, Cambridge, Heidelberg, and Basel, also had Christian origins. The University of Oxford's motto is "Dominus illuminatio mea." It is Latin for "The Lord is my light," which comes from the opening words of Psalm 27.

Chapter 20

Who is Abraham Lincoln?

Abraham Lincoln was the 16th President of the United States. In 1863, during the American Civil War, he issued the Emancipation Proclamation. It declared that all slaves in the rebellious states shall be free. This proclamation affected between 3 to 4 million slaves in those states.

As Lincoln used the Bible as his moral compass,[1] he most likely noted that God condemned slavery. Exodus 21:16 says, "He who kidnaps a man—whether he has sold him or is still holding him—shall be put to death." This quotation is from the Bible commentary *The Rational Bible: Exodus* (Regnery Faith, 2018). The book's subtitle is "God, Slavery, and Freedom." The author, Dennis Prager, explains that this law would have forbidden most forms of slavery.

In Deuteronomy 24:7, God further denounces slavery as evil. It states, "If a man is found to have kidnapped a fellow Israelite, enslaving him or selling him, that kidnapper shall die, thus you will

---

1. Other U.S. presidents also used the Bible as their moral compass. Read President John Quincy Adams's letter to his son about reading the Bible daily. Find this letter at: https://founders.archives.gov/documents/Adams/99-03-02-2021.

sweep out evil from your midst." This Scripture quotation is from Dennis Prager's book, *The Rational Bible: Deuteronomy* (Regnery Faith, 2022). This second verse would have given clarity to Lincoln that he must end slavery in the United States.

In Lincoln's March 4, 1865, Second Inaugural Address, he "communicates that the war is best understood as divine punishment for the sin of slavery." This explanation can be found in the article: "'With Malice Toward None…': Lincoln's Second Inaugural Address' by the National Parks Service. You can find this article by entering "National Park Service Lincoln's Second Inaugural Address" in a Google search.

Abraham Lincoln and Charles Darwin were born on the same day: February 12, 1809.

But their lives could not have been more different. Charles Darwin was born into a wealthy English family. His father was a medical doctor and a successful businessman. His wealth allowed Darwin to enjoy a privileged upbringing. He grew up to be the most famous naturalist in history by writing his book *Origin of Species*.

In contrast, Abraham Lincoln was born in a one-room log cabin. He was the son of parents without formal schooling. Despite his impoverished childhood, Lincoln became one of the greatest presidents of the United States. He changed the course of history by abolishing slavery. A man who studied the Bible, Abraham Lincoln, said, "I believe the Bible is the best gift God has ever given to man." He also said, "All things most desirable for man's welfare, here and hereafter, are to be found portrayed in it."

While Abraham Lincoln lived 150 years ago, his words remain true today. Indeed, Dr. David Berlinski, the American philosopher, mathematician, and writer, states: "The Old Testament is the greatest repository of human knowledge and wisdom in the history of civilization, any culture, any time, any place." Berlinski advises college students to read the Bible. He explains, "Every attitude current today....is discussed in the Bible." (From the Hoover Institution interview "David Berlinski - Atheism and its Scientific Pretensions," April 25, 2011. This interview is available on the YouTube "Hoover Institution" channel.)

Oh how I love your law! It is my meditation all the day. Your commandment makes me wiser than my enemies, for it is ever with me. I have more understanding than all my teachers, for your testimonies are my meditation. I understand more than the aged, for I keep your precepts.

Psalm 119: 97-100

Chapter 21

Are we really an "amazing masterpiece?"

Absolutely! We are astonishingly impressive. In 1871, Alfred Russell Wallace wrote "The Limits of Natural Selection as Applied to Man."[1] He explained that we are so superior to other animals that evolutionary theory cannot account for our development.

Who was Alfred Wallace? Wallace was an English biologist. He conceived the theory of evolution through natural selection at the same time as Charles Darwin. In 1858, Wallace sent his theory to Darwin. When Darwin saw Wallace had the same idea, Darwin rushed to publish his book, *Origin of Species.* But, before his book came out in 1859, an 1858 scientific meeting presented their theory. It was called the "Darwin-Wallace theory."

Like Darwin, Wallace vigorously promoted evolution. Yet 13 years after proposing this theory, Wallace wrote that natural

---

1. This essay can be found in the book *Natural Selection and Tropical Nature; Essays on Descriptive and Theoretical Biology*, Macmillan & Co, 1875. The book is available online at archive.org by searching "Natural Selection and Tropical Nature."

selection (later known as "survival of the fittest"[2]) cannot account for human development.

Alfred Wallace highlighted the incredible superiority of humans over apes in various aspects:

- *Abstract thought:* Humans have enormous intellectual ability. We have capabilities for abstract thought. Unlike other animals, we can reason with abstract ideas. We can create laws and establish governments. We can develop and understand mathematical concepts and explore science.

- *Dextrous hands:* Human hands have opposable thumbs. We have independent movement of all ten fingers. This ability gives us exceptional capability for manipulating our world. Unlike other animals, we can write, create and use hand tools, paint pictures, and play musical instruments.

- *Vocal abilities:* The human larynx gives us unique vocal skills. With our unique vocal tract, we can engage in articulate speech. Wallace writes that we can also produce "wonderful power, range, flexibility and sweetness of musical sounds." Unlike other animals, we can discuss life issues and sing together in harmony.

As humans, we take our abilities for granted.

---

2. "Natural selection" was the term Darwin used in the first four editions of his *Origin of Species*. But, Alfred Wallace suggested to Darwin that he switch from "natural selection" to "survival of the fittest." Wallace felt the term "selection" implied a "selector." Accordingly, Darwin began using "survival of the fittest" in his fifth, 1869 edition.

Why do our distinctive abilities undermine the idea that evolutionary theory can explain the development of human beings?

Wallace says that Darwin takes care to impress upon us that *natural selection can only evolve new adaptive features that help an animal survive in the struggle for existence*. Stated another way, no organ or capability will be developed or retained unless it affords a survival advantage.

Wallace explains that natural selection only produces a *relative* advantage. It cannot create absolute perfection.

Yet Wallace notes that early humans as hunter-gatherers had enormous brain power. Their brain power was way beyond any functional use for survival. Their brains gave humans much more than a relative advantage over other animals. Early humans had latent or unused intellectual abilities. Thus, natural selection could not have developed them.

With our superior brains, perfect hands, voice, and language, we can do many things when fully used. We can create art and music. We can play complex games like chess, invent new tools, and build complex buildings. We can also do mathematics, think philosophically about life, and theorize about abstract ideas such as the law of gravity.

Wallace says it is as if our brain and body were prepared in advance for progress toward civilization. He says we have been given the qualities needed to become spiritual beings.

Although Wallace was Darwin's early partner in proposing evolution by natural selection, Wallace stated:

> The inference I would draw from this class of phenomena is, that a superior intelligence has guided the development of man in a definite direction, and for a special purpose....and we must therefore admit the possibility that, if we are not the highest intelligence in the universe, some higher intelligence

> may have directed the process by which the human
> race was developed.... (p. 204)

We are so much more advanced than other animals that Alfred Wallace reached a remarkable conclusion. He concluded that humans must have been developed by a "higher intelligence" for a special purpose.

Ironically, Wallace was the person who convinced Darwin to use the term "survival of the fittest" instead of "natural selection." He advised Darwin to make this change to avoid suggesting there was a "selector." But later, Wallace realized that evolution could not explain why humans were so advanced.

With his new understanding of humans, Wallace wrote to Darwin. Wallace said he would publish an article explaining the limits of natural selection. Darwin responded, "I hope you have not murdered too completely your own & my child." (You can read Darwin's March 27, 1869 letter containing this quote. Go to the University of Cambridge's Darwin Correspondence Project website: "darwinproject.ac.uk." Then, enter the search term "I hope you have not murdered.")

Wallace saw the extreme superiority of humans over other animals 150 years ago. This recognition contrasts with what some teach today. Today, many scientists claim that humans are not much different from other animals.

And yes, we are not only astoundingly impressive; we are a beautiful masterpiece. In 1869, Alfred Wallace wrote:[3]

---

3. Wallace, A. R. 1869. "Sir Charles Lyell on geological climates and the origin of species." Quarterly Review, 126 (252): 359-394

How did man acquire his erect posture, his delicate yet expressive features, the marvellous beauty and symmetry of his whole external form;—a form which stands alone, in many respects more distinct from that of all the higher animals than they are from each other? ...The supreme beauty of our form and countenance has probably been the source of all our aesthetic ideas and emotions, which could hardly have arisen had we retained the shape and features of an erect gorilla.

The beauty of the human form makes us marvel at Michelangelo's statue of David. And the human body internally is even more awe-inspiring. The cellular complexity and biological processes orchestrating the body's functions are astounding.

Even the most impressive human creations cannot match our body's intricate design. Indeed, geneticist and professor Dr. John Sanford says in his book *Genetic Entropy* (FMS Publications, 2015) that nothing humans create can compare to the complexity of life or even the DNA in our cells.

The Bible says in Genesis 1:27-28: "So God created man in his own image, in the image of God he created him; male and female he created them. *And God blessed them.*"

Each of us is an amazing masterpiece, created and blessed by God.

To challenge the view that we are not very different from other animals, I highly recommend a video titled "The Uniqueness of Man." In this video, Dr. Stuart Burgess explains the unique design of humans. For instance, he describes the irreducible complexity of the human knee joint. This joint allows us to stand upright, unlike other animals. He explains how the human foot is unique. It enables us to balance when standing. He also describes many other remarkable features of humans. You can find his presentation re-titled "How The Human Body's Anatomy Disproves Evolution" on the YouTube channel "Answers in Genesis."

The more I study nature, the more I
stand amazed at the work of the Creator.

-Louis Pasteur

Seeing the Elephant

And you will know the truth,
And the truth will set you free.

John 8:32

Chapter 22
What God Said to Job

The Bible tells a story that highlights another issue with evolutionary theory. In the Book of Job, a once wealthy man named Job suddenly suffers terrible illness and misfortune. He complains bitterly, questioning God's treatment of him. He says:

> But when I hoped for good, evil came, and when I waited for light, darkness came.
>
> My *inward parts* are in turmoil and never still; days of affliction come to meet me.
>
> Job 30:26-27

God replies with anger that Job would dare to question Him. He says that He will now challenge Job with his questions:

> Who is this that darkens counsel by words without knowledge?
>
> Dress for action like a man; I will question you and you make it known to me.
>
> Job 38:2-3

God's challenges include:

> Where were you when I laid the foundations of the earth? Tell me if you have understanding?
>
> Job 38:4

> Have you comprehended the expanse of the earth? Tell me if you know.
>
> Job 38:18

And:

> Who has put wisdom in the *inward parts* or given understanding to the mind?
>
> Job 38:36

By posing these questions, God made it clear to Job that He created the world. He put "wisdom" into our bodies and gave us a mind.

And as we are God's creation, we will never know all the mysteries of life. The Book of Isaiah says:

> My thoughts are not your thoughts, nor are your ways my ways, declares the Lord.

> For as the heavens are higher than the earth, so are my ways higher than your ways and my thoughts than your thoughts.
>
> Isaiah 55:8-9

While the Bible says that God gave "understanding to the mind," Charles Darwin believed that the human mind must have evolved from lower animals. In a personal communication (to William Graham, July 3, 1881), Darwin writes:

> But then with me the horrid doubt always arises whether the convictions of man's mind, which has been developed from the mind of the lower animals, are of any value or at all trustworthy. Would anyone trust in the convictions of a monkey's mind, if there are any convictions in such a mind?

Charles Darwin realized the implications of his theory of evolution. If the human mind evolved by random variation and natural selection, as his theory proposed, then we cannot fully trust our minds. It is like the fact that we would never fully trust a computer or calculator if we knew its programming was developed by random variations.

This communication is called "Darwin's horrid doubt." Dr. John Lennox discusses this quotation in his book *Can Science Explain Everything* (The Good Book Company, 2019). You can read the letter with this quote. Go to the University of Cambridge's Darwin Correspondence Project website: "darwinproject.ac.uk." Then, enter the search term "William Graham 3 July 1881."

Chapter 23

What We Know

Our body's cells contain DNA, a molecular code consisting of billions of characters. Nano-sized molecular machines read the code. They then assemble amino acids into 20,000 proteins. These proteins form the building blocks of our body's tissues. They also run the biochemical processes needed for life (e.g., the hemoglobin protein in red blood cells carries oxygen to the entire body).

The DNA code and molecular machines could not have just evolved from simpler forms. If they existed in less complete forms, they would not function. They are like mechanical watches that would not tell time if one of their gears was missing. The different molecular machines, together, form an irreducibly complex system. All are needed for our cells to grow.

The DNA code relies on fully functioning molecular machines. Without these machines, cells would be unable to divide and multiply. Cells would not make proteins. If cells do not manufacture proteins, there would be no body tissue. Without body tissue, *there would be no organism for Darwin's evolution to influence!*

So, without molecular machines, living creatures would not exist to reproduce and evolve. This fact highlights a significant implication: Because "evolution" can only occur *after* DNA and molecular machines create living creatures, evolution cannot explain the pre-existence of DNA and molecular machines.

> Think about the different cell phones you see in stores. Initially, programmers and engineers worked hard to create the software and electronics for each new model. Then, engineers designed factories to build these cell phones.
>
> When these cell phones enter the market, some become popular because they have cool features. But the ones that sell poorly get discontinued. It is like the "survival of the fittest" for cell phones—only the best survive. However, this idea does not explain how cell phones were invented or made. They were designed, engineered, and created by intelligent engineers.
>
> So, it does not make sense when evolutionary biologists say that evolution explains DNA and molecular machines. It is like saying "survival of the fittest" among cell phones somehow created the computer code inside them and designed the factories that made them.

When we examine the complexity of DNA and molecular machines, it is clear to any rational person that they could not have simply come about by chance. Creating instructional code is a logical, structured process. The design of machines requires careful engineering. The intricate processes by which molecular machines assemble our body's proteins point undeniably to a "higher intelligence."

As a result, we can conclude that a higher intelligence than ourselves exists. There is a Creator who intended for us to exist.

We are not just accidents of nature but are "fearfully and wonderfully made" (Psalm 139:14).

The creative genius of using molecular machines to read our genetic code to transform our digested food into our bodies is amazing. We are the only generation privileged to have the intricacies of our creation revealed to us.

It is so incredible that it is not surprising that these discoveries have won Nobel Prizes. But, the scientific community and media have yet to recognize their significance. It is time for the scientific community to embrace the fundamental truths that:

- DNA "is like a computer program but far, far more advanced than any software ever created," as Bill Gates writes, and

- DNA's code "is the language in which God created life," as the President of the United States, Bill Clinton, declared.

It is time for scientists and the media to stop crediting "evolution" for the beauty and diversity of the natural world.

Know that the Lord, he is God! It is he who made us,
and we are his; we are his people, and the sheep of his pasture.

Psalm 100:3

Chapter 24

Revealing the Path of Life: Three Questions

This book presents two possible views of our world. Evolution is one view. If you wish to hold this view, it requires accepting the following:

- Abiogenesis. You believe that simple chemicals spontaneously self-assembled themselves into organic components. The organic building blocks then formed into proteins despite incredibly miniscule odds. These proteins combined with other components and became a cell. Genetic code inside the cell created itself.

- The first cell, likely a bacterium, replicated. Over millions of years, it became a tiny, mobile, worm-like organism, then a creature with legs, until it became a human being. Your earliest ancestors were, therefore, likely to be germs and wiggly creatures.

- You accept evolutionary explanations that your DNA's instructional code and molecular machines also evolved through survival of the fittest. You must ignore that the pre-existence of DNA and molecular machines is necessary for replicating life and that replicating life is required before Darwinian evolution can even begin.

- You deny the existence of irreducible complexity in living things as it is an inconvenient truth.

- To search for the truth about life, you must confine yourself to exploring physical processes and the material world. Rational explanations beyond these constraints must be excluded. You are here because of evolution and survival of the fittest, an accident of nature.

- Your mind evolved from a monkey's mind through random chance. Given that your brain developed by random mutations, you cannot trust your thoughts, calculations, or judgments.

- As God did not create you, no one has any right to set moral standards for your life. You are free to do whatever you like.

- As just another animal on planet Earth, your life has no more intrinsic value or rights than any other creature. "Survival of the fittest" means that the strongest can enslave or harm you if that is their wish. You have the freedom to act likewise.

- You can enjoy holding views in line with the National Science Teaching Association and the scientific establishment.

The other view is a Biblical view. If you wish to hold this view, it requires accepting the following:

- You have inherent worth because God created you.

- Your ancestors were human beings. You and your ancestors were brilliantly engineered.

- Your body's DNA and molecular machines that built all your body tissues and manage your body's biochemical processes are not a mystery to you. God said he created your inward parts.

- You can marvel at the irreducible complexity of God's design. Whether it is the flight of birds, the molecular DNA untangling machine called Topoisomerase, or the thin-film interference that creates the beautiful iridescent colors of peacock tail feathers and Siamese fighting fish, you can appreciate the beauty of his work.

- In your quest for the truth about life, you can be open to considering all rational arguments, even those beyond physical processes. You are here because your parents wanted you to be or God wanted you to be.

- You can trust your thoughts, calculations, or judgments because God gave you a mind.

- As God created you, your life has a purpose, and you live within the moral boundaries of your Creator.

- If you live in the United States, you can embrace the words of its 1776 Declaration of Independence. It states: "We hold these truths to be self-evident, that all men are created equal, that they are endowed by their Creator with certain unalienable Rights, that among these are Life,

Liberty and the pursuit of Happiness."

- You must tolerate holding views that are frowned upon by the National Science Teaching Association and the scientific establishment.

Three Questions

Now, with these two competing worldviews in mind, consider how you would answer the following three questions:

Q1. What world would you choose to live in?

A) Charles Darwin's world: A world created by no one.

B) Abraham Lincoln's world: A world created by God.

Q2. Charles Darwin and Louis Pasteur were both influential scientists in the 1860s. If your world could have only one scientist, who would you choose?

A) Charles Darwin, who traveled the world to study nature and wrote the *Origin of Species* to explain his theory of evolution by natural selection. Proposing that all life descended from a common ancestor, his theory could explain the diversity of life. He became the world's most admired scientist.

B) Louis Pasteur, who was a chemistry professor, pharmacist, and microbiologist. He proved that life arises from life, developed pasteurization to kill microbes in milk, and invented vaccines using weakened pathogens. Considered the "father of bacteriology," his discoveries saved millions of lives throughout history.

Q3. Imagine that you entered a time machine, and it is now February 12, 1809. You are told that instead of both Darwin and Lincoln being born that day, there would only be one birth. You could be born as either Charles Darwin or Abraham Lincoln. *You are told that your choice will alter the course of history.* Which person would you choose to be?

A) Charles Darwin, the son of a wealthy doctor and businessman, who grew up in a large mansion and attended the University of Cambridge. Without a need to work for money, he could sail the world and study nature. His theory of evolution revolutionized how the natural world is viewed. He lived until the age of 73. His body was buried in England's Westminster Abby, along with other distinguished figures in literature, politics, science, arts, and royalty, to honor his scientific achievements. (One does not have to believe in God to be buried there despite it being a church.) Today, he is considered the most famous and one of the most outstanding scientists ever.

B) Abraham Lincoln who grew up in a one-room log cabin. His parents were farmers without formal education. With only a year of formal schooling,

Lincoln studied books and rose from poverty to become the 16th President of the United States. He led a nation through a civil war that saw over 600,000 deaths. But he gave freedom to over 3 million slaves. Like some other outstanding leaders (India's Mahatma Gandhi, Egypt's Anwar Sadat, and America's Martin Luther King Jr.), Lincoln was assassinated. His life was cut short at the age of 56. A grateful nation created the finest memorial ever to an American: The Lincoln Memorial. It is the most visited memorial or monument in the United States.

Your answers to these three questions reflect how you choose to view the world, what you value in other people, and how you see yourself in the world. They reveal who you are and who you will be. They reveal your path in life. It is a choice that each of us is allowed to make.

❧

You make known to me the path of life;
in your presence, there is fullness of joy;
at your right hand are pleasures forevermore.

Psalm 16:11

Chapter 25

Greater Love

As the author of this book, I feel I must offer an apology for presenting three questions in the previous chapter. I wrote this book so its readers can stand firm in their Christian beliefs, knowing the truth in a world blinded by evolutionary views. With this in mind, the purpose of Chapter 24, titled "Revealing the Path of Life," concludes the book by addressing the ultimate meaning for each of us. The final hypothetical question, asks you to choose between being born Charles Darwin or Abraham Lincoln. It is deeply personal. Readers choosing to read this book would not have expected it. The question may be uncomfortable, and for that, I apologize.

Please allow me to explain further. The question of choosing between being born as Darwin or Lincoln is inherently challenging. It presents a "false dichotomy." This question limits you to two vastly different choices. In reality, we have many choices about how to live our lives. Nevertheless, the question forces us to examine our values.

Indeed, after writing the question, I had to think deeply to find my own answer. Would I be willing to endure hardship and a life cut short to give freedom to over 3 million slaves and end slavery? Being born into wealth like Darwin, traveling the world to study nature, and living a long life sounds much more attractive. But, the fact that I would be spending my life promoting a false theory and one that would turn people away from God would be too difficult to swallow.

In today's society, the pursuit of wealth and fame is widespread. Attaining riches or fame, including making significant scientific discoveries, is seen as a sign of success. Many people, if not most, would choose to live the life of Charles Darwin.

However, the eminent psychiatrist Dr. Alfred Adler,[1] known for describing how feelings of inferiority affect a child's development, offers an important truth. Dr. Adler says that *if our life pursuit is self-centered and not guided by an interest in serving others, our striving will be a precursor to failure in life—whether it is in having meaningful work, satisfying friendships, or love and intimacy*. We can see the truth of this statement when we consider teenagers who join gangs or self-obsessed celebrities embarking on their fourth marriage.

From a Christian perspective, Jesus says that the most important commandment is first to love God and then to love our neighbors. The Book of Matthew states:

> "Teacher, which is the great commandment in the Law?" And he said to him, "You shall love the Lord your God with all your heart and with all your soul and with all your mind. This is the great and first commandment. And a second is like it: You shall love your neighbor as yourself. On these

---

1. While most people have not heard of Alfred Adler, they may be familiar with his term "inferiority complex" and the idea that birth order influences a child's development. Dr. Adler emphasized that we must all feel a sense of belonging, and how we view the world and our place in it affects the development of our personality.

two commandments depend all the Law and the Prophets."

Matthew 22:37-40

Loving your neighbor as yourself demands that we care about other people. According to Dr. Adler, caring for others in our relationships and our broader community is a value that is key to a meaningful, successful life. So when we encounter moments of difficulty in our relationships or work, we must ask ourselves, "Am I solely focusing on my own needs and feelings? Or am I considering how to help the other person or contribute to serving others?" By answering this question, we can determine whether the problem stems from our lack of concern for the other person's needs or if the problem genuinely lies with them. On a broader scale, we should consider the sentiment expressed by President John F. Kennedy's famous words spoken at his 1961 inauguration. He said, "Ask not what your country can do for you—ask what you can do for your country."

Beyond loving our neighbor, the difficulty in choosing between being born as Abraham Lincoln or Charles Darwin is the extent to which we are willing to sacrifice our own lives for the welfare of others. In war, a soldier jumps on top of a grenade to save fellow soldiers. Many parents would sacrifice their own lives for their children. Jesus went to the cross and laid down His life for the sake of all.

Yet, as written in Matthew 26:39, Jesus prayed at Gethsemane before facing the cross, saying: "My Father, if it be possible, let this cup pass from me; nevertheless, not as I will, but as you will." To willingly sacrifice one's life for others is not easy, but it is the greatest love of all. According to John 15:13, in the words of Jesus:

Greater love has no one than this,
that someone lay down his life for his friends.

Chapter 26

My Prayer for You

Now that I am talking to you as personally as possible, allow me to pray these words.

Dear God, the Creator of all things and every cell of my body, thank you for bringing this reader to this book. I pray that through these pages, readers gain an unwavering conviction that they are your holy and magnificent creation and that they can confidently stand firm against the views that men and women are mere accidents of nature.

You state in Jeremiah 33:3, "Call to me and I will answer you, and will tell you great and hidden things that you have not known." I pray that readers call upon you with all their heart and soul and that you give them the understanding they seek.

As teenage readers prepare to enter the secular world, I pray they will hold your words of Joshua 1:9 close to their hearts: "Have I not commanded you? Be strong and courageous. Do not be frightened, and do not be dismayed, for the Lord your God is with you wherever you go."

In addition, I pray that readers will see the wisdom in the Bible. I pray that they come to believe, like Abraham Lincoln, that the Bible is the best gift God has ever given to man. And I pray that through the Bible, readers understand that not only were they created by you, but by accepting Jesus as their savior, they will be blessed and have eternal life with you.

Lord, I also pray for parents who are giving this book to their teenagers. I pray that they see your hand in their children's journey and that you will guide their children's path in life.

In John 21:15-17, you asked Peter three times, "Do you love me." And after Peter replied three times, "Yes Lord; you know that I love you," you said to him, "Feed my lambs," "Tend my sheep," and "Feed my sheep."

Lord, we know that you love us as parents. You blessed us with our children. Just as you asked Peter to care for your sheep, we ask that you feed our lambs and tend our sheep.

We pray that, in your holy hands, our children can never be lost and will run to you when you call.

In the name of Jesus Christ, we pray.

Amen.

ele

Then they said to him, What must we do, to be
doing the works of God? Jesus answered them, "This is the
work of God, that you believe in him whom he has sent."

John 6:28-29

Thank You & A Request

Thank you so much for reading *A Teen Girl Answers Darwin*. I appreciate your time and hope it was meaningful for you. As an author, I would love to hear your thoughts.

Could you please take a moment to leave a review on Amazon? Your feedback will help other potential readers determine if this book is suitable for their families.

Your support means a great deal to me and I am grateful for every reader.

With heartfelt thanks,
Kelvin Chan

Student Activity Package & Poster

Homeschooling parents, youth group leaders, and teachers can download a Student Activity Package. This package consists of a fun quiz designed to reinforce learning and crossword puzzles.

To thank you for buying this book, I would also like to offer you a digital download of one of my Beatitude posters. It highlights Matthew 5:8: "Blessed are the pure in heart for they will see God."

You can access these downloads at this link:
www.raisealife.com/downloads

Thanks again!

Suggested Reading

For those interested in learning more, here are additional books and references.

1. *Darwin's Black Box: The Biochemical Challenge to Evolution*. Michael J. Behe. Free Press, 1996.
   The author, a professor of biochemistry, argues that many biochemical systems, such as molecular machines, could not have evolved because any less sophisticated form would not have functioned at all. He calls this concept "irreducible complexity."

2. *Hallmarks of Design (2nd ed.)*. Stuart Burgess, Day One Publications, 2002.
   This book uses the author's professional expertise as a professor of design science to show that design in nature reveals a designer. It is a valuable resource as it explains the irreducible complexity of human knees, peacock tail feathers, and bird flight. The author describes many fascinating details, from the incredible features of hummingbirds, camels, and platypuses to the unique design of man. The book highlights evidence of design that evolutionary scientists prefer to avoid acknowledging. I highly recommend this book. (Available at www.dayone.co.uk)

3. *The Hidden Face of God: Science Reveals the Ultimate Truth*. Gerald L. Schroeder, Free Press, 2001.
   Gerald Schroeder is a scientist with expertise in physics and the biological sciences. He explains that the essence of the physical world and life is information and the wisdom of God. I recommend this book for advanced science students.

4. *Metamorphosis: The Beauty and Design of Butterflies.* (DVD) Illustra Media, 2011.
   This DVD beautifully presents the spectacular migration and lifecycle of Monarch butterflies. By seeing the fantastic complexity of their lifecycle, the viewer will be awed by the improbability of evolution. I highly recommend this DVD.

5. *The Rational Bible: Deuteronomy*. Dennis Prager, Regnery Faith, 2022.
   Dennis Prager has now published three books in his series, *The Rational Bible*. They are *Exodus* (2018), *Genesis* (2019), and *Deuteronomy* (2022). He states that in the past, the Bible was "the primary vehicle by which parents passed wisdom on to their children." I recommend this series of books as they helped me appreciate the wisdom of the Bible, the Judeo-Christian roots of the English and American justice systems, and our ethical or moral beliefs.

6. *Signature in the Cell: DNA and the Evidence for Intelligent Design*. Stephen C. Meyer. HarperCollins, 2009.
   The author explains that the sophisticated code in DNA is "information" and functions like a software program. The code is so complex that it would be impossible to have arisen by random chance. As science has been unable to uncover the source of such biological information, and

human experience tells us that the mind is always the creative source of information, one can infer that DNA is evidence of an intelligent designer.

7. *What if Jesus Had Never Been Born?* D. James Kennedy and Jerry Newcombe. Thomas Nelson, 1994.
Tom Holland, the historian who wrote *Dominion: How the Christian Revolution Remade the World* (Basic Books, 2019), says that we are a society of goldfish swimming in a Christian fishbowl. In the West, we grow up in a culture shaped by Jesus and Christianity, but we do not know it, just as fish do not know that they are swimming in water. The book *What if Jesus Had Never Been Born* details the enormous impact of Jesus on our world today. I highly recommend this book.

8. *Wonders of Creation: Design in a Fallen World*. Stuart Burgess and Andy McIntosh. Master Books, 2018.
Two engineering professors describe a panorama of features in our natural world to demonstrate design. The book covers land animals, birds, insects, and even humans. Photographs, diagrams, and commentary highlight evidence of design that evolutionary scientists prefer to avoid acknowledging. I highly recommend this remarkable book.

For wisdom will come into your heart,
and knowledge will be pleasant to your soul;
discretion will watch over you,
understanding will guard you.

Proverbs 2: 10-11

Acknowledgments

I wish to thank God for giving me this dream and a specific purpose in my retirement. It is wonderful to feel that there is something important that I need to do each day and have something to look forward to.

I am also thankful for the scientists who courageously write and explain the scientific evidence for creation and why the evidence does not support Darwinian evolution. I would also like to acknowledge the work of the organizations that create the educational YouTube videos offered for further reference.

On a more personal note, I am grateful to those who helped me with this book. These individuals include my cousins Lister and Larry, who reviewed early drafts and gave me suggestions, and reviewers of the manuscript, including Dr. Stuart Burgess, Dr. Andy McIntosh, and Dr. Bryan Born. I would also like to thank Melissa for her feedback, scientific review, and editing, Gordon for proofreading the final manuscript, and Rebecca, who created the cover illustration. Finally, I would also like to thank Pastor Rick and my wife, Phui Fun, for their support and encouragement.

About the Author

Kelvin Chan grew up in Victoria, British Columbia, where his paternal grandmother taught him the Bible. A daughter of a physician evangelist spreading the gospel in Hong Kong, she came to Canada in 1911 as a young bride for a Christian man and to raise a family.

When Kelvin was five years old, his grandmother would tell him a different story from the Bible each day, from Genesis to the Gospels. Like other children, he enjoyed stories and did not take them seriously. It was not until late in life, after he married a Christian wife and had two daughters that he came to believe and was baptized.

Kelvin began his professional career at two colleges. He taught psychology and led a counselor training program. Returning to university for a business degree, Kelvin switched to a career in management. He worked as a business analyst and a market researcher. He also held management positions in product development, market research, and data analytics.

Upon retiring, Kelvin renewed an early interest in photography. His photography is dedicated to conveying the Christian message. His landscape photography includes posters illustrating the Beatitudes from the Book of Matthew.

Turning to writing, this is his first book, which he wrote for his two daughters and all of God's children.